Index Funds

Index Funds

Strategies for Investment Success

Will McClatchy
IndexFunds.com

John Wiley & Sons, Inc.

Contents

Acknowledgments

Indexing is by no means a new practice, and those of us who are more recent converts are beholden to pioneers for paving the way, colleagues who work with us to achieve our goals, and members of the community who add insight, assistance, or just a good stir of the pot.

John Bogle, William Sharpe, and Burton Malkiel are among the many pioneers we should be thankful for. Here at IndexFunds.com, we especially appreciate the early work of cofounders Jeff Troutner and Matthew Roberts, who helped launch the site. Then there are the many excellent financial professionals who add so much value to our community, including ever-present Larry Swedroe, site co-founder Jeff Troutner, Bylo Selhi, Rick Ferri, and Steven Evanson, to name a few. Most important are our many energetic regular visitors who help inform newcomers and swap insight and data.

For assistance with this book I want to thank Assistant Editor John Spence, who did most of the original data gathering and who edited the manuscript more times than he cares to remember.

I dedicate this book to my mother Jean and father James, who instilled in me a love of discovery that no doubt brought me to this curious juncture.

Preface

I felt compelled to write this book for the novice index investor for the same reason I started IndexFunds.com. I felt most investors were slowly being taken advantage of by Wall Street, and they needed to know why and how to act in their best interests.

Index investing, or indexing, is the practice of investing broadly in stocks and bonds without attempting to pick winners. Indexers tend to invest "passively" for the long haul with relatively little trading and with few brokerage, fund, and advisory fees.

This practice is by no means a fad, but rather has 30 years of history of actual investment success. This success is predicted by theory and studies from the world's finest economists. Promotion is the only weakness of indexing, and we are trying to do our small part in that area with this book. Traditional financial media feed off the vast flow of fees and profits from actively managed funds and services, whereas the indexing media must content itself to survive on a trickle from the much more lean indexing industry. Few journalists focus almost exclusively on indexing, and we feel that most financial writers do not give it the proper exposure it deserves.

Like many indexing enthusiasts, I encountered this philosophy almost by mistake when I parked some cash in the Vanguard S&P 500 Fund for lack of better ideas. The notion of tying my future financial prosperity to a broad market average such as the S&P 500 sat well with me, but I had no idea how solid the evidence was for that action. Soon after I read with

fascination *Bogle on Mutual Funds*, by John Bogle, founder of the Vanguard Group of mutual funds and considered the father of indexing.

In years of covering business and technology as a journalist I never
met an investment professional who claimed there were easy pickings in
the marketplace, unless they were brand-new to the game. So many managers and advisors are educated, experienced and competent. How to tell
the star among them?

Any journalist who covers investments briefly notices how a good
track record for a few years or even five could make a mutual fund manager into a star. My knowledge of statistics also led me to conclude that
these star managers might be outliers, i.e., lucky.

At the same time I personally knew two stock analysts earning millions of
dollars a year covering high-technology firms with frothy valuations during
the mid-1990s. They were making their mutual fund clients a bundle by
picking Internet and telecommunications winners. I doubted whether I would
pay such individuals such exorbitant sums for just their analytical skills, but
I couldn't help but concede that their picks were making lots of money for
their clients—at the moment. When the crash did come, funds invested in
such stocks recommended by these analysts were decimated (see Figure P.1).

FIGURE P.1   NASDAQ-100 INDEX, 1990–PRESENT

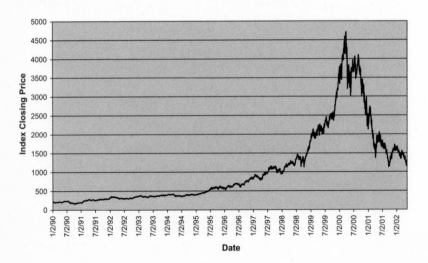

I also felt compelled to write this book because of how reputable media have ignored personal finance. It is not hard to find accurate, timely, and in-depth coverage of most areas of civic life. But in personal finance—something so central to a person's practical freedom and independence—sloppy thinking, hype, and disinformation is rampant. I am not sure that another media article on a subject such as political fundraising reform is going to really make a difference. So many good articles have been written that the public knows about as much as it cares to on this issue by now and will vote its conscience. Likewise for a wide variety of civic issues.

In contrast, the average individual does not know much about index funds, which are the logical extension to the proven buy-and-hold philosophy. Very little is written about indexing, and much of what is written is irrelevant or even factually incorrect. This affects investors individually and collectively. No country can afford to squander its resources for long without suffering for it.

Index or passive investors have their moment when it all seems to make more sense and they are hooked for life. Mine came after a conversation with a stockbroker of extensive experience, an excellent reputation for modest fees, and a practice of recommending conservative stocks for the long term. I learned that his handpicked portfolio of large company stocks rarely deviated much from the Standard & Poor's 500 index of large company stocks and tended to trail just slightly. On average, the portfolio seemed to trail the benchmark by just about the same amount as his fee.

One day I asked him as a business proposition could his clients justify paying extra fees if they rarely deviated from but generally underperformed the market? His astounding answer: "They hire me because they have someone to call and hold their hand when the market goes down." In other words, it was O.K. if he was a minor obstacle to performance, because he would be there to console them! If this broker, who was forthright and sincere, could not see the irony of his words, then perhaps the investment community is infected with a culture of blindness.

I quickly joined the ranks of millions of persons who believe that Wall Street is systematically failing to represent the interests of investors in a way that harms them subtly but materially. Although the art of indexing can be a bit dry and involves numbers and jargon, if retiring with sufficient funds to live comfortably or if saving enough to pay for a child's education is a desirable goal, it should be of interest to everyone. It has a human dimension. Mismanagement of personal finances is detrimental to investors trying to pay for their children's college, retire at a reasonable age, or set aside funds for a rainy day. It has a real effect on real lives.

—Will McClatchy
San Francisco, CA

PART I

The Philosophy of Indexing

CHAPTER 1

Everyone Needs a Benchmark

Like all of life's rich emotional experiences, the full flavor of losing important money cannot be conveyed by literature.[1]

—Fred Schwed, Jr.

No matter how you invest, at some point you must answer the question: "How well have my investments done?" This only can be answered by comparing your portfolio's assets to some reasonable benchmark of similar assets. To disregard how your portfolio performs against other similarly constructed portfolios cultivates ignorance and invites disaster. You may be perennially behind the average investor, but you will never know until you compare.

In the financial world comparisons are made through benchmarks called *indexes*. An index is typically a group of stocks thought to be representative of a certain segment of the market. Each index provider uses different methodologies to determine that market segment. There are literally hundreds of public indexes covering every type of investment, or asset class, imaginable. From large U.S. stocks to bonds to small international stocks and even precious metals, there is an index that tracks them.

In the United States, the Dow Jones Industrials and the Standard and Poor's 500 (S&P 500) are examples of the better known U.S. indexes.

> "An index is a basket of stocks or other assets, and its return is the total return of its components."

Indexes are quite easy to understand. Unfortunately, the majority of investors misunderstand the basic principles of financial comparison. Some resist comprehending out of fear for what they might learn through performance comparisons. Most are misinformed deliberately on this critical subject by financial professionals. As we shall see throughout this book, these professionals have good reason to fear thoughtful comparison of their performance.

A disheartening number of investors mislead themselves. Faced with concrete facts and advice from the best minds available, they reject commonsense indexing solutions in favor of speculative, actively managed funds. Pride, greed, thrill of adventure, and envy are among the emotions that trick them into these mistakes. One of the great tragedies of capitalist nations is that a substantial number of persons who work hard and generate income early in their lives never invest it properly and end up with far less wealth than they could have had at retirement.

Out of the study of comparative performance has grown the investment strategy of indexing. This subtle investment philosophy seeks to grow wealth in a steady, powerful, and efficient manner. The fundamental principle of indexing today calls for investing with appropriate market indexes and not attempting to actively beat them. It settles for the average right up front and rejects the lure of stock picking and market timing. The strategy is often called *passive* investing, in contrast to the *active* management and investing that dominate most funds. This approach not only shuns picking individual stock and bond winners, it also favors keeping trading to a minimum to push down transaction costs.

Far from being mediocre, this philosophy shows consistently better returns with far less risk over time than actively managed investing. Why? Because it takes unnecessary speculation out of investing and keeps expenses and taxes to a minimum. It may not have the wild run-ups where it outdistances others, but it also does not suffer disheartening declines where it falls far behind other investors.

> "It is an undisputed fact that most investors underperform the market average."

Indexing is not a fad or scheme. Hundreds of billions of dollars are indexed today in both retail and institutional funds. This comes to well over a trillion dollars globally. Most observers believe indexing and passive investing will continue to grab market share from active investing for many years to come.

Retail investors trail their institutional peers in adopting this discipline, as is to be expected. It's a strategy for "smart money." Indexing requires a little investment in time and effort to understand. Institutional investors and their consultants have read the literature and examined the data. They have deep financial backgrounds and much more experience. They do not invest based on flashy television campaigns. However, individual investors are catching up fast. The Vanguard S&P 500 Fund is the second largest mutual fund in the world, and it is a virtual certainty that it will soon beat out Fidelity's Magellan Fund for the top spot.

The two major ways to use indexes to measure financial performance meaningfully should be kept separate. They are:

1. Using indexes to compare asset classes (such as stocks versus bonds) and
2. Using indexes to compare a portfolio of stocks against its entire class (such as a mutual fund against an appropriate index).

The first type of comparison is useful in the asset allocation phase of portfolio construction. It acknowledges that it is comparing an apple to an orange and seeks to view differences in this light, including differences of return and of risk. The second type of comparison is useful in judging the performance of fund managers. Unfortunately, most investors and indeed many professionals do not distinguish between these two basic uses, and it makes for unpleasant surprises. Risks may be wildly different between

FIGURE 1.1   CHART OF NASDAQ AGAINST S&P

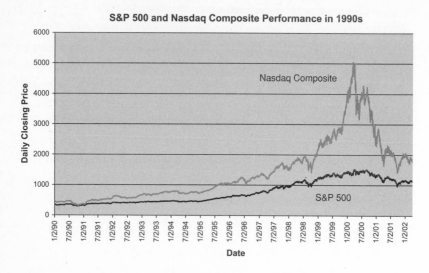

asset classes, as investors find out later when their portfolio has tanked. "But I just wanted a better return!" they may say, which is entirely the point. A better return generally involves higher risk.

Consider how investors eagerly poured money into technology stocks in the late 1990s, thinking that as long as they were "beating the S&P" all would be fine (see Figure 1.1).

Far too many discovered that the assets of tech stocks were fundamentally far more volatile than stocks in the S&P, where there were plenty of oil refiners, car manufacturers, and other relatively stable firms.

When tech stocks tanked, investors blamed their mutual funds for picking the wrong stocks. In all fairness, they should have blamed themselves (or their financial advisor if they had one) for placing too many eggs of one color in the basket. The tech funds do what they are supposed to do, invest in tech stocks. The investors and their financial advisors are the ones who failed to understand the risks of the assets they owned. This is not an indexing versus active investing issue so much as an issue of sensible selection of assets. Luckily, indexing helps the investor focus on that task and take responsibility, whereas delegating that crucial task to an active money manager simply papers over the decision.

Time and time again, one hears an investor or fund manager claim: "My small-company fund did better than the S&P 500 this year. See how I beat the market." This person is comparing apples to oranges. The S&P 500 is a large-company index fund. Because small-company and large-company sectors of the market tend to vary somewhat from year to year, it is very common for one to beat the other in any given year. It means nothing. It is like saying that short skirts are out of fashion. Not to worry. They will come back. If a small-company fund beats an index of smaller companies such as the Russell 2000, then perhaps the fund manager has bragging rights that year. However, most professionals choose to avoid any real education of investors in comparative performance.

> The first question any investor should ask a fund manager is: "What index are you trying to beat?"

It is universally acknowledged that stocks in one industry tend to move up or down as a group more than stocks of other industries. The stock of a hotel company will tend to move in lock step with other hotel companies more than it will with cement companies. When they compare apples to oranges, Wall Street professionals must know what they are doing. A surprising number of investors accept these claims as valid. For fund investors, a comparable index is the benchmark that your fund managers should beat if you are to believe their success was due to superior stock picking.

The key word here is *comparable*. In order to make any meaningful use of an index as a benchmark, it is essential that an investor find an index that contains similar types of assets. Indexing does not just mean investing in the Dow Jones Industrials or in Standard & Poor's 500! This bears repeating because so many investors think these two indexes represent the entire market. These two indexes are perfectly legitimate and useful but are by no means representative of all publicly traded stocks. You will find no small and very few midsized firms in these proprietary indexes. In the S&P, for instance, the average market capitalization is $20 billion! Also, it contains no international stocks, bonds, or real estate investment trusts. The Dow is comprised of only 30 stocks selected by the editorial staff of *The Wall Street Journal*. Despite its longevity and popularity, most investment professionals regard it as a poor overall measure of U.S. large-company stocks.

> Introduced in 1896, the Dow Jones Industrial Average was the first index that sought to track the overall performance of the U.S. economy. Although the benchmark still enjoys immense popularity with the public, it is considered by most financial professionals to be too undiversified. It contains 30 blue-chip stocks across industries selected by the staff of *The Wall Street Journal*.
>
> The S&P 500 was introduced in 1957 and became the recognized standard gauge of the U.S. economy. It is a capitalization-weighted index of 500 companies chosen by a committee for market size, liquidity, and industry group representation. It is estimated that over $1 trillion resides in index funds hitched to the S&P 500.

Most investors discover index investing after a serious disappointment with a star mutual fund. Because indexing is the practice of not choosing star funds but rather settling for the average market return, this is the natural place of refuge for the disheartened. The story often goes like this: Investors read a financial magazine in which a mutual fund is rated four or five "stars" for its ability to outperform a market in recent years. The fund is a hot commodity, so its management can charge a high fee, nearly 2% of assets per year. (It is no surprise that most fund managers grow rich from the fees they charge investors, not on performance of their own investments.) Just as the fund becomes popular with this investor and many others, the market turns in another direction. The type of companies favored so heavily by the fund in past years built too many factories too fast. As new capacity for production came on line, customers who had rushed to buy the products now have all they need. Price wars break out as competitors try to land the few new customers available to the industry, and profits plummet. One or two of the key stocks the fund or broker has loaded up on collapse, and most soften. The rest of the market also dips but not nearly as much as the star fund.

The investors lick their wounds and wonders why their star manager is being left behind by others.

Meanwhile, the fund or broker continues to collect the management fee unapologetically. Every spring during tax preparation, investors' tax accountants note that they are paying unusually high capital gains because many investors pulled out, forcing the fund to sell stocks and record capital gains from past years' returns that these investors never enjoyed. All this while the fund is down. Talk about a double blow! After enough of this investors begin to feel that a great track record is not necessarily a good predictor of future returns and that beating the market is not so important as matching it. When they sell, they are more careful about asset selection and they choose an index fund. The danger for this type of indexer is being too shy to move beyond dominant indexes out of fear of once again being left behind. Diversifying into indexes of smaller domestic or international stocks may make sense.

Many other investors stumble into indexing when they park assets into an S&P 500 fund (or other dominant broad index in their country) for want of another idea. They never get around to doing anything more with it and move on to other aspects of their lives. Even on the occasional year when the index is beaten by a majority of active funds (actually an apples to oranges comparison in most cases), investors seem content enough that at least they are in good company. Most investors will have shared the same fate.

If they have a larger portfolio, they are probably already diversified into several funds representing numerous equities and they start replacing their active funds with index funds, one by one. Come tax time, their accountants report that their capital gains distributions are quite small and likely to stay that way until they recoup their investment. It soon dawns on them that they are committed indexers. These indexers-by-default might benefit from learning more about indexing alternatives. As the portfolio grows, it may be a good idea to diversify to indexes that contain smaller U.S. companies and even international equities.

Less common are indexers who thoroughly investigate the concept at the beginning of their investment career. These individuals are the types who read nutrition labels on the back of food packaging and read up on their symptoms in medical texts before going to see the doctor. They read books on indexing, compare management fees closely, and pay attention to long-term tax gains. They study differences between indexes and learn about exchange-traded index funds, relatively new indexing tools that will be discussed later. The pitfall for these persons is allowing their research to delay investment decisions and becoming enamored with overly complex portfolios. It is important to keep portfolios reasonably simple and act with relative speed. No matter what type of investor you are, learning a bit about indexing will give you clarity when faced with a flood of financial data and a few key decisions.

> Indices or indexes? Proper English conjugation for more than one index is *indices,* but U.S. investment professionals tend to use *indexes* for simplicity. English investors on the other hand, avoid the problem by using the word *tracker*!

There is no more important question for the individual investor than: "Can I beat Wall Street with confidence?" Given enough attempts, any person can "beat the Street" for you, that is, pick stocks that perform better than the market, but you can also walk into a Las Vegas casino and come out a millionaire that evening. Why is it that gambling with your life savings is more respectable than gambling in a casino? Well, it is at least true that most equity funds go up over time, no matter how they underperform, whereas most gamblers lose all over time. Still, the relative underperformance is the same as one might expect from playing roulette.

Luckily, although ignorance concerning indexes is the norm, becoming a proficient indexer is relatively easy. It is certainly far less difficult than becoming a good stock picker or predictor of which star fund will perform best. The decision to index automatically evaporates a whole host of chores brought on by active management. There is no money manager to select, just asset classes to choose. The mere task of knowing what asset classes you own is vastly simplified. Portfolios with multiple active funds are often anyone's guess as to how much large-cap value, mid-cap growth, etc., it contains. All that information is instantly known with a portfolio of index funds, and, of course, indexers walk away forever from onerous management fees.

There are many valid approaches to indexing and many strong new products coming onto the market every year, so the open-minded indexer need not be restricted to a single preferred indexing philosophy or set of products. However, some approaches, indexes, and products appear to have obvious weaknesses. It is essential to steer clear of them. To that end, this book is divided into two parts, one for contemplation of the issues and one for action.

Part I of this book leads the reader to the main issues and debates concerning indexing and offers evidence and anecdotes to keep in mind. Part II provides a path of action for indexing with example portfolios, comparisons of indexes, descriptions of index funds, and details of portfolio maintenance tasks.

I begin in Chapter 2 by laying out a commonsense view of the standard tenets of passive and index investing. Above all, this version of indexing encourages open-minded examination of new ideas and products and discourages dogmatism and the blind acceptance of data-driven arguments. In this chapter I describe the profile of successful indexers as we have encountered them, including the general philosophy needed, underlying motivations, and discipline required.

It is important for the investor to understand the nature of Wall Street's dominant ethos, that of active stock picking and frantic buying and selling. In Chapter 3 we examine how Wall Street operates, not always for the full benefit of the investor. Yes, stocks are a particularly strong and, over increasingly long periods of time, not terribly risky way of accumulating wealth. However, they are far more so when an investor steers clear of exorbitant and standard Wall Street fees. The fact is that Wall Street professionals are not entirely on your side. Sure, they help you invest but not in the most effective and efficient manner. They take their cut, a big cut, for very little actual useful work. We will show why it is naïve to believe that investment professionals won't try to sell unnecessary and expensive services. Investing should never be free, but it need not be so expensive. When it is, it is detrimental to investors. Luckily, it is not hard to recognize symptoms of the high fee/star manager disease that will suck your wealth away. Quarantine against such disease is the best defense.

It is equally important for the newcomer to get a sense of how index investors filter out the phenomenal amount of noise emanating from the financial markets and media. This is addressed in Chapter 3 before the onslaught of charts, data, and economic debate. In Chapter 4 we examine the financial media and suggest how to listen, and just as importantly, how to ignore various parts of it. From television to newspapers to Web sites, most media is noise. We point out the good, the bad, and the ugly.

In Chapter 5 we discuss what some of the brightest thinkers say on the subject. These include Nobel laureates and other leading economists who do not derive their income from active Wall Street funds. They all agree stock picking and other active strategies are of dubious value. That's right, virtually no serious economist believes that on average attempting to pick stocks or hiring someone to do it will result in superior results, especially after fees. Almost every thinker who has studied the area will tell you that fees, and to a lesser extent, taxes, are the crucial obstacles to achieving average performance, and the higher the fee the harder it is to catch up.

We follow with a cursory review of economic theory that impacts indexing in Chapter 6. This area is vast, so we cover it in outline form. Luckily most pertinent theory can be boiled down to a few precepts and explained in fairly concrete terms. We take a pause in Chapter 7 to juxtapose the two largest mutual funds in the world, one actively run and one an index fund. Fidelity's legendary Magellan Fund and Vanguard's S&P 500 Fund make for a fascinating comparison.

In Chapter 8, we examine serious studies comparing the performance of active funds against indexes over many years. There are many such studies, and we present a small sample with as little financial jargon as possible. Their message is quite clear: Stock picking and active trading is largely wasted effort.

A number of tenacious myths have made their way into investors' psyches, fueled in large part by Wall Street marketing dollars. In Chapter 9 readers may want to check to see whether they hold any easily debunked preconceived notions about indexing.

Next comes the weighing of risk versus return in determining asset allocation. Chapter 10 is really the meat of indexing. Choose markets with the right risk/return profiles, and you have done most of the work. Individual asset classes follow, and Chapter 11 explores the nature of indexes of bonds, large-company stocks, midsized equities, small-company stocks, and international stocks, among other possible choices.

In Chapter 12 we confirm why expenses are the ultimate long-term determinant of performance. This is truly the root of the problem in investing today. Management expenses, transaction fees, and sales commissions are the triple-headed monster dragging down investor returns. Actual returns over time, of course, are net of fees and sales commissions. The more fees you pay, the less that net return will be; because many active mutual funds charge 1% to 2%, this can really add up over time, especially with the effect of compounding.

Taxes, last but not least in Part I, need to be kept in mind. In Chapter 13, we see that taxes play an important role in disposable net income, to the detriment of the active investor and to the benefit of the indexer. Delaying taxes is the name of the game. If you pay taxes at a later date, you can use the money in the meantime to earn more.

In Part II of the book we turn from learning about indexing to actually executing it. A financial plan is highly encouraged as a first step, so in Chapter 14, we walk through this subject briefly with an eye to indexing. Questions such as, "How much do you need, when, and with how much certainty?" must be answered. Rules of thumb are offered, and links to on-line resources are included.

Selection of indexes is the next decision item. In Chapter 15 we present major indexes for various asset classes. Most are appropriate for the typical investor, but there are important differences.

At this point it may help to view some typical model portfolios designed for persons at different stages in their life. Younger persons, for instance, should probably put a greater percentage of stocks in their portfolio than older individuals who are nearing retirement and have less time to wait out a sharp drop. Various model portfolios are presented in Chapter 16.

An important new class of index fund called the *exchange-traded funds* is so different from the traditional mutual fund that it needs to be discussed separately. It can be bought and sold instantly unlike the mutual fund, which is bought at the end of the day and generally held for years. Because it entails transaction fees but has very low expenses and a favorable tax profile, the question of whether is it less costly overall will be addressed in Chapter 17.

At this point investors are ready to pick a fund of some sort or buy stocks themselves. In Chapter 18 we list all of our favorite funds sorted by asset class. We list fees and discuss their strengths and weaknesses. Frankly, there are so many excellent choices it's an indexer's delight. Mutual funds, exchange-traded funds, and enhanced index funds are all presented. Even building your own index is described.

Maintaining your index portfolio is not hard. The primary maintenance activity is so-called rebalancing, where the portfolio is brought back to the original ratios between asset classes that were chosen in the initial asset allocation. Chapter 19 leads you through this commonsense tune-up action taken once a quarter or even once a year.

Overall, I encourage open-mindedness for the learning indexer. There is a sizable contingent of experienced indexers who have become somewhat rigid in their thinking. They seem uninterested in considering new strategies and alternatives. After following, writing on, and sometimes participating in debates at *www.indexfunds.com* on just about every issue concerning indexing for several years now, I am increasingly hesitant to side absolutely with any school of thought. Important new theoretical approaches, data, financial products, and tactics for implementation of portfolios are emerging every day. This discipline is still very much in its infancy. As it so often is in other disciplines, the debate is not so much about the correct answer for this or that burning question. The issue is often whether we have asked the right question, and for that we should maintain a healthy skepticism.

CHAPTER 2

Commonsense Indexing

"If I knew how something was going to play out, I'd be in New York picking stocks."

—Rick Majerus, University of Utah basketball coach,
on who would win U.S. NCAA college basketball
national tournament

Indexing is an updated version of the buy-and-hold approach to equity investing. This proven philosophy says, "Find good companies that represent good economic value and stick with them." Invented before indexing was available in fund form, buy-and-hold has all along been quintessential passive investing. After disgust with wild speculation early in the 20th century, mainstream investors forced the buy-and-hold approach onto Wall Street. Investors simply wouldn't stand for wild speculation and huge fees.

Historical results of buying and holding U.S. stocks are hard to argue with (see Figure 2.1).

Note some of buy-and-hold's key tenets:

- Find a solid asset

- Buy at a fair price

- Trade infrequently

FIGURE 2.1   GRAPH OF HISTORICAL RETURNS

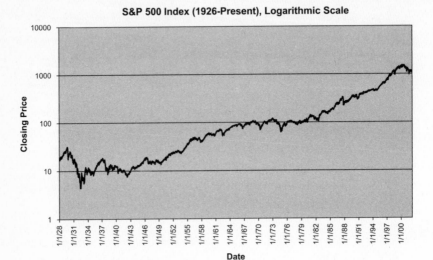

S&P 500 Index (1926-Present), Logarithmic Scale

- Keep costs down

- Don't time markets

Probably the only element added by indexing is the removal of individual stock picking and the introduction of vast diversification. In the early half of the 1900s, when buy-and-hold gained sway, there was no way around individual stock picking. The breadth of diversification simply wasn't practical for many investors, who paid fairly steep brokerage fees to own shares. There were no on-line brokers back then! Also, mutual funds hadn't established their wild popularity of today. If you are a buy-and-hold stock investor, indexing is the natural evolution for you.

THE CREED

Indexers live and invest by a creed that accepts reality and shuns fantasy. They accept the normal cycles of nature, which is generous to the patient individual. Indexers do not concern themselves with the success of others and therefore do not view investing as a contest. Psychologically, indexers are generally calm and centered and rarely anxious. It is enough to take reasonable steps to achieve their financial goals. If certain others pass them by, so be it. Freedom is the greatest luxury, constraint the greatest annoyance. Not achieving one's goals is a great danger, whereas exceeding one's reasonable goals is not so great a benefit.

Consider workers who have diligently saved for retirement and look forward to the day when they may travel, pursue hobbies, spend more time with family, and simply take it easy. If these persons who have looked forward so many years to these activities were to be kept back by a star mutual fund that stumbled, this indeed is a tragedy. These persons have experienced loss of freedom, intolerable in the modern world, and they must now continue to work even as they grow old or be content to scuttle plans for relaxation and travel they so looked forward to.

Consider on the other hand workers who strike it rich, who are lucky enough to find one of the few equity funds that exceeds the market average after fees. They have exceeded their goals. So what? It is an event to be celebrated, but can it change their life to so great an extent? This is doubtful. Lack of freedom for not attaining one's financial independence when it is easily achievable through average market returns is inexcusable, and yet millions of investors continue to do it.

Indexers and passive investors have a set of values distinct from frenetic market timers and traders. The indexing investor values transparency, consistency, patience and peace of mind.

Indexing can be simple, but it is not simplistic. Indexers often perform a thorough examination of all the asset classes at a point in time for their risk profiles and expected income. This may not be necessary or even appropriate for many individual investors, but for the large pension plan it is almost a requirement. It is imperative to spend money researching what exactly is in the portfolios and what might happen to different asset classes in various situations.

Not every aspect of indexing is appropriate for every investor. They should be matched with the level of sophistication that they understand and can practice with comfort.

Commonsense indexing invariably agrees with traditional commonsense investing. It further supports them with evidence and provides a framework for implementing them. Buy-and-hold has long been a thread of wisdom on Wall Street. It's just that it is not practiced in a very disciplined way by the buy-and-hold practitioners in the actively managed world. Indexing reinforces this notion with theory, evidence, and attractive products to support it.

My main criticism of indexing as it is practiced today is its excessive reliance on certain arguments depending on historical returns. Although well-meaning, this has tended to make the practice of indexing rigid. Historical reliance on numbers is important but dangerous when investment decisions are based upon this analysis alone. Predictions based on possible outcomes and scenarios also are to be contemplated, but generally predictions in the matters of men and nature have turned out to be rather poor. It turns out that predicting the markets has a lot in common with predicting other fields including the weather, population growth, the future of technology, and development of industries. The conclusion of William Sherden, who examined each of these fields in *The Fortune Sellers,* a book examining the business of prediction, was that it is largely a sham.[1] Predictions may hold water for the short term, but for the longer term, where it really matters, there is precious little benefit. Money, time, and energy are clearly wasted in such efforts.

With weather, for instance, even great advances in computational power in supercomputers have failed to crack Mother Nature. Weather prediction still begins to break down at about three days. The possible combinations of results of storm activity many hundreds of miles away are entirely unpredictable. Even if computational power continues to increase at its prodigious rate, many meteorologists doubt that predictive ability is likely to exceed four days anytime soon without some new fundamental scientific insight of which we are not now aware. Of course, that may well happen, but if it does it will be discontinuous; that is, the meteorologists will know about it first (and profit from it if they can), and television viewers of meteorologists during the news hour will find out about it dead last. The change will happen suddenly. All of a sudden, weather predictors with new knowledge will have a new edge in storm warning and everyone else will be one hour (or one day if the breakthrough is huge) behind. Those weather predictors who do not have early knowledge of the new theory will be left behind. The same thing happens in the stock market. When breakthroughs occur, the average investor is unlikely to benefit in the short term from any new radical insight. The pros will skim the cream and sell the rest.

Futurology, or the business of predicting tomorrow's technology, is in the same boat. Flying cars, videophones, and men on Mars will all occur, but when has been quite hard to predict for the leading futurologists. Likewise with predicting population growth. It's of intense interest to the United Nations and to insurance companies, but no one seems to be able to do it well. Corporate planning of trends that will affect a company also has been a bust. Inevitably new product developments or factors coming from outside a company's industry arrive to take everyone by surprise.

TYPE OF PREDICTION	PERIOD WHEN PREDICTIONS BREAK DOWN
Weather	About 3 days
Technology	5–10 years
Population	10–20 years
Investment	Almost immediate

Above all, common sense should be relied upon. There is no formula for this. The traditional debate between active versus passive investing tends to involve a barrage of past returns data. Investment professionals are quite good at sifting through this data to find the figures that prove their point, but investors should remain wary. Common sense must be the guide of all reasonable investors. Thankfully, common sense is amply supported by economic theory. Concepts such as reversion to the mean, essentially a rule of thumb that warns that outsized performance is likely to return to average, is heavily supported by financial statistics. It has only modest predictive power and so has been ignored by the dominant active crowd on Wall Street, but it has shown itself to be a powerful warning signal against risky speculation.

Investors tend to stick to investment plans that make sense to them at a gut level. Investors may be convinced briefly of an investment approach by clever arguments, but unless they embrace the philosophy behind it they will tend to switch to another approach when the next clever argument is made. They will not see patterns in the financial world that explain so much of how Wall Street operates and make indexing so compelling. They will be overwhelmed by the flood of conflicting information concerning the markets and possible strategies. If investors index, they will do so without conviction, easily swayed back to active investing when a sweet-talking active money manager or broker comes along. It's not enough to simply do it, you have to understand why you're doing it.

At the height of the Internet bubble many were warning of its impending doom. The average buy-and-hold investor was affected because of the increasingly large percentage of indexes these firms occupied. It was hard to escape them. Some overconfident souls were predicting exactly when it would occur, but many sensible individuals were giving general warning of its possibility or even likelihood. The case for an impending disaster was laid convincingly in Anthony and Michael Perkins's 1999 book, *The Internet Bubble.*[2] They predicted devastating losses to Internet company stockholders. It was all the more remarkable because of their background as founders of *Red Herring,* a magazine that follows Internet and other high-technology start-ups. They surely lost some friends in that industry, but they were right.

Other thinkers, including Wall Street professionals and economists, were echoing these predictions for other growth firms, including traditional software and telecommunications. It's not as if the possibility of excessive stock valuations in 1999 and 2000 were a secret. Yale University professor Robert Shiller warned investors in early 2000 that they were witnessing the "biggest [stock market] bubble ever in this country."[3]

A myopic, formulistic thinker would have discarded these warnings as unscientific. Returns of the past are the best predictor of the future, according the formalist, and the rest is subjective guessing. Even after formalists' portfolios were sorely punished in subsequent years, surprisingly many still clung to the notion that no one could have known that the technology bubble was a bubble and not a precursor to endless growth for Internet start-ups. This argument is logical, but lacks common sense. As this book relates, experience and study has shown that it is hard to predict even general outcomes and impossible to consistently predict precise ones. But common sense dictates that the prudent investor should step aside in particularly frothy times. All I can say is that I side with common sense over formulaic thinking.

MANY WAYS TO INDEX

There is a misconception among some indexers that one must select this or that reputable index and invest in a fund that tracks it perfectly. Nothing could be further from the truth. The largest and most sophisticated institutional indexers in the world willingly stray somewhat from the highly publicized indexes. They are not worried about being slightly off the beaten path. They are more worried about racking up unnecessary transaction fees and generating taxes. The essence of indexing is to find a reasonable approximation of attractive assets and to invest in them cheaply and simply.

That is why indexing is so often termed *passive investing*. It is not so much how you do it as how calmly and elegantly (and efficiently). Here elegance is often described as the minimal amount of fee drag and tax consequences, hence the emphasis on keeping transactions to a minimum.

Indexing is a little like diving. There are extra points given out for complexity and sophistication, but only if done with grace. A simple maneuver done well is preferable to a difficult one poorly executed. In investing the key is to leave as little splash as possible, and you do get points for elegance. Really, both investors and investment professionals are at fault: investors for not asking simple questions and reading bestsellers describing this state of affairs, and investment professionals for not challenging the status quo and demanding fairer treatment for their clients, even at their own expense.

Brokers or advisors should provide counsel to a client as they would to their own family member. Unfortunately, that is not often the case. The way most investors and investment professionals go about doing business is wrong because it does not take into account true interests of the investors. Institutional investors have long known about this state of affairs. Many investors are becoming aware of this or they would not have gradually made the Vanguard S&P 500 Fund one of the two largest mutual funds in the world.

However, many more still do not understand the power of indexing. "Indexing is seen by some investors as an obscure quantitative technique, with investment decisions made in a 'black box' rather than by a real person," wrote PriceWaterhouseCoopers in a 1997 survey of indexing. "Emotional factors may continue to constrain more widespread acceptance, even as better information on indexing becomes available."[4]

CHAPTER 3

Is Wall Street
on Your Side?

*The evidence shows that if the market can be beaten in
picking individual stocks, it is damn hard to do, and the
vast majority of investment professionals fail trying.*

—William A. Sherden, *The Fortune Sellers*[1]

The investment industry exists to help you increase your wealth, and to make a profit (probably a little too much profit) for itself along the way. The average mutual fund, for instance, takes out 1.42% out of your account every year, in good markets and bad. Compare that to the 0.08% to 0.4% that the leading index funds charge for various types of domestic equities. The prudent investor has to ask the question: "Is this a fair charge and do I have to pay it?"

Wall Street is not against the investor, but neither does it have your interests foremost at all times. This should not surprise anyone, nor is it a reason to do any finger-pointing. Wall Street is in the perfectly valid business of selling financial services, and it's hard to expect the marketplace for capitalism be less than enthusiastic about its services. Caveat emptor; let the buyer beware.

Wall Street believes that the more services you buy, the better off you are. How many of these services are necessary or lead to demonstrably higher returns? Not as many as most people think. Financial services are different than any other because their whole purported goal is to enhance net wealth—they are not goods or services to be consumed or utilized for direct benefit. Spending more money on financial services is not like spending more money on a car. With more money, a car buyer generally will get a proportionately better car. In financial services, spending Cadillac money may still get you a Chevrolet, and probably an economy model at that.

The reason is simple. The more you spend on fees, advisors, brokers, commissions, and the like, the less you have working for you. To make up for the amount you spend on extra services, you have to outperform the market just to break even. Wall Street services don't guarantee you higher financial returns, only the hope of higher financial returns. The whole goal of investing is to have the most money at the end while taking the least amount of risk. Generally, higher fees force investors and their fund managers into buying riskier stocks that perform better on average but with much less certainty, settling for a worse overall return, or hoping that the extra services somehow deploy assets smarter by finding better performing stocks that are no less risky than the average.

The professionals with proven track records claim they can "beat the Street." We will examine this claim throughout the book, but until you have seen the evidence, you should regard it as no more than a claim. In the meantime, the working hypothesis ought to be that a bare minimum of financial services is necessary, and that anything more than that remains suspect until justified by reliable data. For some curious reason, Wall Street has convinced investors of the opposite: The full range of financial services are necessary, and any proposal to scale back should be scrutinized heavily.

Doesn't every business try to up-sell its customers to a better model? I don't think Wall Street is any more or less forthright than other industries. After all, in the capitalist model there is no maximum level of consumption. It is as much as the consumer can afford or be convinced to spend. It would be remarkable indeed if the investment industry was the only industry that refrained from selling high-priced services because lower-priced ones will do. Do clothing manufacturers sell last year's fashion just because it is less expensive to keep cranking out the same styles? No, they encourage new styles and charge handsomely for them. Customers can see instantly that they are getting a fundamentally different product and gladly pay more for it. With most goods, consumption is not about preservation and enhancement of capital. It is unfair to blame Wall Street entirely for pursuing its own interests.

The key figure that indexers watch is the relative difference they can make with low-fee funds versus high-fee ones.

Buying mutual funds and exchange-traded funds that own broad indexed portfolios of stocks can be quite cheap. What is not cheap are the full-fare fees of actively managed funds that Wall Street wants to sell you. Compare for yourself the annual management fees of these leading active mutual funds (see Table 3.1).

These examples are quite typical. Without question, some assistance is probably necessary for any investor, and Wall Street feels more help is better than less. Of course, more service costs more money. By using traditional high-fee Wall Street investment services, you will no doubt grow your wealth over time, but not as fast, on average, as if you had ignored Wall Street and invested in indexing products.

TABLE 3.1   ACTIVE VERSUS PASSIVE FUNDS

ACTIVE FUND NAME	TICKER	NET ASSETS $MM	EXPENSE RATIO
Fidelity Magellan	FMAGX	77766.9	0.88%
Janus	JANSX	24757	0.83%
American Funds Income Fund A	AMECX	20223.6	0.62%
Putnam Fund or Growth & Income A	PGRWX	19630.5	0.81%
PASSIVE FUND NAME	TICKER	NET ASSETS $MM	EXPENSE RATIO
Vanguard 500 Index	VFINX	70981.1	0.18%
SPDRs	SPY	28840.7	0.11%
NASDAQ 100 Trust Shares	QQQ	22178.1	0.20%
Vanguard Total Stock Index	VTSMX	15699.1	0.20%

SOURCE: Morningstar data as of 3/31/2002

Clearly, every investor needs a brokerage house or mutual fund if they are to own a broad portfolio of stocks and bonds. It is pretty difficult to buy stocks on your own, and for as little as $7 an on-line brokerage will do it for you. So mutual fund brokerage firms are the indexer's friend. But does every fund investor need to pay high mutual fund fees to participate in stock market booms? Does every investor need to pay full retail brokerage fees for buying and selling stocks or funds? The indexer says no. Generally experienced indexers opt for efficient brokers, that is to say competent and cheap.

Personal stock brokers are very helpful for executing trades on complex asset classes, and they provide an important convenience for busy or less computer-literate individuals who do not like on-line brokerage houses. However, as a source of general investment advice they offer two problems. First, they are often compensated on the sale of products they don't believe in or understand. Even with active mutual funds, what appears to be an annual fee often contains a sales commission spaced out over many years that clients never find in the fine print. Just as I was finishing the manuscript to this book, I had a short conversation with a telephone broker about mutual funds. "We don't make money on no-load funds, so that's not something we recommend," he told me flatly. It would seem the clients' interests were not foremost at heart, but he was surprisingly candid about it. Clients who wanted no-load funds could easily find them on his firm's Internet site, he cheerfully explained. His job clearly was to push loaded funds, and he was doing it with laudable candor.

The second problem is that brokers are often focused and trained primarily for execution of trades for a wide variety of products, not for planning an asset class review. They simply aren't as focused on the investor's primary mission, that is, picking some good asset classes and keeping trading down. Their clients need them to know a little about every kind of asset, and it makes it hard for them to focus on any single one.

There has been an important shift in recent decades that can be for better or worse. Many brokers bill clients with a "wrap" fee that makes them almost indistinguishable from financial advisors. An increasing minority of brokers from major brokerage houses are willing to put their clients in portfolios of index funds with low costs and few trades, even though this means fewer fees for themselves. These types of brokers are on your side.

But if they work for a major brokerage house, often they will be pressured to lean more to active funds with hefty fees that quietly pay commissions to the brokers.

Although better trained than brokers for the task, securities analysts are also problematic as a source of advice. They have very clear conflicts of interest in the debate. No era better illustrates this than the late 1990s. When the telecom, Internet, and computer stocks were going up, no one could question the wisdom or bias of relentlessly bullish analysts. Only when these stocks crashed and destroyed many a retirement portfolio did a wider awareness spread of a well-known conflict of interest. The same investment banks that employ analysts to judge the worth of a stock are also trying to sell these firms lucrative IPO (initial public offering), merger, and other investment banking services. It was well understood that the firm that could best help energize a stock on its analysis side was the front-runner to get investment banking deals.

Investment clients reading stock reports certainly weren't paying for the multi-million-dollar salaries. These clearly were paid out of the flood of money from the other side of the investment bank. The Enron bankruptcy of 2002 was simply the straw that broke the camel's back. Analysts were so blinded to its shenanigans by fear of offending powerful management and of being browbeaten by investment banking colleagues that many U.S. politicians called for federal regulation of analysts.

Probably the one position in the financial industry that is most needed and least filled is the pure financial planner. Everyone should have a financial plan, it only has to be done once a decade or so, and it can cost as little as $500. It is money well spent. The problem is that there are so few pure planners. Most "planners" are actually brokers or financial advisors or insurance salesmen who do planning to bring in clients for their other products or advisory fees. There is nothing wrong with that, as long as your intentions are clear. You, the client, just want the plan and will interview separately for any other services and intend to manage your indexed portfolio at low cost. It is understandable why there are so few pure planners. It is hard to justify spending marketing dollars to get a new client who is not likely to return for years for a new plan. Financial advisors are an obvious choice for assistance and more available, certainly for portfolio review or initial financial planning.

The one financial professional you can probably trust the most, the certified public accountant (CPA) is also the least leveraged by the investing public. Of all the financial professionals available to investors, CPAs are the least biased. Although they often refrain from dispensing specific financial recommendations, that is not what is in short supply. Claims and predictions abound; sound and unbiased analysis concerning these claims does not.

CPAs can confirm figures in this book and other texts, are inherently skeptical of get-rich-quick schemes, and are well aware of tax effects of various investment strategies. Their fees are almost always by the hour or project, and their work is tangible and generally devoid of marketing fluff.

As a professional class, CPAs tend to listen more and talk less than most. Accountants are trained to ferret out the excessive assumptions underlying a rosy projection, read fine print about onerous costs, and uncover outright fraud. They are not trained to make projections or assess asset classes. That is actually a positive. It means they generally will not attempt to pump up any one asset class over another, except to perhaps warn against inflated assets. They seem to be naturally conservative. Not to be forgotten, they understand taxes better than other financial professionals.

If you actually figure out the fees for a solid CPA, it is quite cheap. Even at $100 to $200 per hour, in three to five hours even the most well-heeled investors will have all the professional advice they need on the effects of their portfolio. Most investors can get by on an hour or two. Without intending to be, the CPA is the natural ally of indexing and always a handy person to have on hand for taxation issues, where detail is best handled by a specialist. Lastly, the CPA can help build a financial plan if no pure planner is available. If there is sufficient money at stake to justify freeing up a certain amount of cash, my advice is to engage a CPA at least for tax planning and occasional feedback on a portfolio.

An unrecognized benefit of the indexer's outlook is how calming and liberating it is. In a small way it improves the quality of life of the investor. The behavior of investment professionals and the pattern of their claims become recognizable. Statements by reputable economists are easier to grasp. Everything seems to make sense once you examine the economic and historical context of the indexing versus active debate. On a practical level, not everyone is so numbers-oriented. These arguments just don't seem to stick long with certain individuals, even if they agree in principle initially.

Not Necessarily Dishonest

To say that Wall Street is not entirely on your side is not to say that financial professionals are dishonest. The mature indexer understands that very few professionals engage in self-serving practices such as frenetic buying and selling (called "churning") in client accounts to generate commissions, by recommending investments from which they get unusually large sales commissions, or even by embezzling. These practices do happen, especially in environments where brokers or fund managers have discretionary power to pick stocks. Removing this small possibility is indeed a minor argument for indexing, especially for the busy or less knowledgeable individual who might not notice how they were being taken advantage of. However, that is not the main reason to avoid Wall Street, because most of Wall Street is honest in the strict sense.

It is far more doubtful whether Wall Street truly has the investor's interests at heart. In many cases, Wall Street professionals are so brainwashed that they don't even see their bias. Many truly believe they provide a valuable service even when they perennially underperform the markets. Over time indexers like me tend to feel the same way about Wall Street professionals as many businesspersons feel about lawyers. We need good ones, and well-paid ones, but maybe not quite so many well-paid ones!

Like any professional, brokers and active fund managers have every right to try to earn their fees by trying to convince investors of their value to the investing public. But investors also have every right to say no, and today most are abdicating that right. Occasionally I hear a stockbroker or financial advisor get defensive and say, "I have only my investors' interests at heart and would never sell them a service they don't need." You rarely hear them concede that perhaps they have an inherent bias and self-interest at stake that might blind them to the truth. You never hear them say, "Here are all the extra fees I am charging you that I am going to make up in your account so you can at least match the market." Only a tiny fraction of funds or money managers agree to work on a performance basis, where you pay for transaction expenses but nothing more unless you exceed certain targets.

The point is not that Wall Street wants you to lose money. Investing with high-fee mutual funds probably will grow your assets substantially over time. For instance, if your actively managed stock fund returns 10.5% per year over the long run and you pay 1.5% in fees, you still make out with a 9% annual return. That means doubling your money every nine years. However, had you paid a more reasonable 0.5% in fees, you would have doubled your money a year sooner.

CLOSET INDEX FUNDS

While the debate rages about the merits of active versus passive, for many famous funds the discussion is irrelevant because they are almost indistinguishable from the benchmarks they attempt to beat. They contain most of the same stocks in similar amounts and move closely with the benchmark. Actually, there is one big difference: Active funds charge significantly more than the index funds they quietly imitate.

Indexers derisively call these sheep-in-wolf's clothing "closet index funds." At IndexFunds.com we saw so many closet index funds that in 2000 we decided to examine the largest U.S. active mutual funds for imitative behavior. In Table 3.2, we show some truly egregious examples, including some popular funds that charge hefty sales loads and annual

TABLE 3.2   ACTIVE VERSUS PASSIVE FUNDS

NAME	NEAREST INDEX	R-SQUARED (100% = INDISTINGUISHABLE)	SALES FEES	ANNUAL EXPENSE RATIO
Fidelity Magellan	S&P 500	95%	Front: 3%	0.50%
MFS Emerging Growth B	Wilshire 4500	81%	Deferred: 4%	2.91%
Putnam Growth & Inc A	S&P 500	84%	Front: 5.75%	1.04%
Merrill Lynch Capital B	S&P 500	87%	Deferred: 4%	2.59%
Vanguard 500	S&P 500	100%	None	0.18%

Reprinted by Permission of IndexFunds, Inc.
SOURCE: Morningstar

management fees, followed by the alternative to most of them, the inexpensive Vanguard S&P 500.

The key statistic describing similarity, R-Squared, is the percentage of a fund's movement that can be mathematically "explained" by movements in the benchmark index. R-Squared results for these funds range from 81% to 95%, with the worst example being Fidelity's Magellan. It deviated only 5% of the time from (it is just as likely to have underperformed for that 5% of the time as outperformed) from the S&P 500, and yet it takes in hundreds of millions of dollars each year.

STOCK PICKING AS ENTERTAINMENT

Admittedly, investing is a dry affair, and stock picking helps perk it up a bit. It's probably the only sexy aspect of Wall Street. It has drama, personalities, and mystery. The thrill of watching the bears and the bulls clash every day is fascinating. Unfortunately, as entertainment it can get expensive.

A high fee just raises the bar and makes it even harder for the mutual fund to keep up with the index fund. Some funds respond with more advertising, others by moving into riskier investments, and still others by aggressively starting numerous "seed funds" in hopes that a few will outperform the market and be "stars." Stock picking is the least productive activity on Wall Street, but it takes up an enormous amount of energy and expense. However, as long as customers demand this activity in such copious amounts, Wall Street will happily oblige.

Active investing creates inherently less diversified portfolios. By definition, active portfolios that concentrate capital in certain stocks are more risky than ones that spread it out. If a portfolio has more than 100 stocks and no more than 2% to 3% in any one, then the danger is lessened. But plenty of funds load up on one, two, or three stocks with 5% positions.

The active investment game is inherently more expensive to play than the passive one. Wall Street charges more for stock picking, and indeed they have to. They have expensive star managers, research analysts, and often large advertising bills to tout their excellent team.

The level of detail involved in stock picking is astonishing. One must read the balance sheet and income statement carefully, watch closely for announcements and even rumors, go to management presentations, and consider the future growth prospects of the company. There is a reason that individual stock analysts concentrate on one industry. There is simply too much to know about an industry, and the players, to be able to pick one stock over another. One must get to know the products, profit margins, boom-and-bust cycles, new innovations, and a myriad of other details. Analysts frequently spend their lives trying to understand industries such as oil or computers—and freely admit they are still learning.

To investors depending on analysts' recommendations, the difference between an alert analyst in the stock-picking universe and one who is a little slow to react can be devastating. Stock picking is inevitably more labor-intensive than buying the whole market. For this reason low-cost investing and indexing are inextricably linked. Before buying any pricey service, the indexer always asks, "What am I getting for all that expense?"

The indexer notes that an active mutual fund charging 1% more than its index counterpart has to outperform that index fund 1% year-in and year-out just to stay even. Most funds don't even attempt to justify their fees. It is taken as a given that the investor must pay. Curiously, most investors see it that way, too. Unlike the rest of the economy, where improvements in computers, telecommunications, and management practices have lowered costs while raising product quality, in the mutual fund community fees are actually rising (see Table 3.3).

These costs are largely attributable to distribution and marketing.

THE MARKETING TREADMILL

Most of the investment services industry is stuck in a kind of marketing treadmill whereby funds run very hard to stay in place and investors foot the bill. Even mutual fund managers that hate it must run on this treadmill as fast as they can in order to compete for business. Increasingly, it appears to dispassionate observers that Wall Street is making its money through marketing and brand building, not by creating wealth for their investors. A huge amount of marketing money, paid for by investors, is spent trying to convince investors that this or that fund can beat the market. How can such expenditures help investors who foot the bill?

TABLE 3.3   AVERAGE EXPENSE RATIO OF DOMESTIC
            EQUITY FUNDS

YEAR	EXPENSE RATIO	# OF FUNDS
1992	1.31%	980
1993	1.29%	1301
1994	1.35%	1686
1995	1.39%	2114
1996	1.39%	2627
1997	1.39%	3335
1998	1.42%	4181
1999	1.43%	4886
2000	1.44%	5341
2001	1.47%	4739

SOURCE: Morningstar

Investing is made to seem complicated because the markets are complicated. This is used to justify high fees. In fact, investing in markets can be
made very easy with indexing.

"SEEDING AND WEEDING"

The marketing treadmill is not just a promotions game. It actually reaches
deep into the operations of funds themselves. Because fund performance
is so hard to predict, and because the pressure is so great to have a top
fund in any given quarter, fund groups are obliged to do what is called
"seeding and weeding."

Seeding is the practice of starting small new funds every year with the
express intent to spread out in every different direction. It doesn't really
matter what strategies fledgling funds take, so long as they are all radically
different. This will assure the fund group that at any given time it will have
a hot new winner. Since one can't predict what the hot new sector will be,
the chance of having a hot young fund in a year or two is directly propor-

tional to the number that are started. From these seeds a few stellar performers will emerge and attract fresh investment cash.

Weeding is the practice of merging the assets of the inevitable losers into the winners at opportune moments before they get too big, thereby hiding much of the losing record of the fund group. The losers are culled, usually by being merged into the winners. Investors themselves are relieved to finally have their money folded into a winner. Everyone is happy. This practice is so pervasive that active fund groups are virtually obliged to do so, because if they don't they will not survive in the active fund marketing wars. Not surprisingly, there has been a huge expansion in the number of funds, from about 1200 domestic stock funds in 1991 to about 4800 in 2002.[2] It is doubtful that even half will survive 10 years. The growth of new funds is not limited to enterprising little boutique investment firms with special expertise and vision. Large firms churn out new funds as a matter of course. Indexers often talk about "seeding and weeding" of funds in the abstract, which does not convey the financial wreckage created by these practices.

One of the most glaring examples of a firm bringing investors late to the party and sending them home with a headache is Merrill Lynch, the giant brokerage firm. In September 1998, its sole tech offering was Merrill Lynch Technology, and the fund was ranked in the bottom tenth of its peers for the trailing one-year, three-year and five-year periods, according to Morningstar. Management was replaced in 1998, and shortly after, Merrill created Merrill Lynch Global Technology (MAGTX) and merged Merrill Lynch Technology into it.

Then Merrill Lynch Internet Strategies (MBNTX) Fund was launched in March 2000, no doubt in response to client demand to chase returns of high-flying technology stocks. It opened its doors with a breathtaking $1.1 billion in assets. Within 12 months it lost 74% of its value, according to Morningstar. In October of 2001, only 19 months after opening its doors, it was merged into Merrill Lynch's Global Technology Fund.

Another Merrill loser was the Merrill Lynch Growth Fund (MBQRX), which tanked with the Nasdaq in 2000 and 2001. In late 2001 it was merged with the larger Merrill Lynch Fundamental Growth Fund (MCFGX), which was doing well among its peers at the time. It doesn't stop there.

On March 25, 2002, Merrill planned to merge Merrill Lynch Premier Growth B (MBPGX) and Merrill Lynch Mid Cap Growth A into Merrill Lynch Large Cap Growth A (MALHX), which was a strong performer relative to its peers.

The records of these losers are erased from memory by almost everyone and are not counted by most journalists describing historical returns. This will continue to be the case as long as fund companies can bury the performance of poor-performing funds with periodic weeding. You won't see this sort of behavior at the Vanguard Group or Barclays' Global Investors. Indexers tend not to complain about much to the fund manager. After all, they got what they asked for!

The inevitable carnage from constant creation of new funds in every conceivable investment direction to ensure a few winners cannot be in the best interest of investors. Seeding and weeding has added a boost to average remaining active returns that is often called *survivorship bias*. As we shall see later, legitimate comparative studies must account for the poor records of defunct funds as well as the stellar ones of funds that kept their doors open.

Some investors don't pay professionals at all to pick stocks. They do it themselves, but that doesn't remove the cost. These "day traders" still work very hard to match the market, much less beat it. The ones that I have met seem nerve-wracked. Day traders who say this activity is cost-free are not counting the opportunity cost of their time spent. They could have been earning income during that time doing something else, and they really should ask themselves honestly whether they have the depth of resources or expertise to pass judgment on stocks from numerous industries.

Of course, index funds and professionals that promote them are human, too, and have their own interests at heart. It's just that industry leaders in index funds take so much *less* away from the customer. To be sure, some firms do charge onerous fees for indexing products and services.

Morgan Stanley has an S&P 500 index fund with a 1.50% expense ratio, according to Morningstar. Typically, such fund owners are active fund groups sold through traditional brokerage houses that encourage stock picking. Typically, they do not prosper. The funds stay small, because most indexers do their homework and seek out low-cost funds.

Advisors who recommend indexes can be quite costly. Some charge clients 1% or more of assets just to manage a simple retirement portfolio the clients could construct themsleves. Even when discounts are applied to larger accounts, advisor fees can cost investors dearly over time. Financial advisors are increasingly well educated and understand the benefits of low-cost indexing for their clients. Not all, however, feel that their fees should be lowered to benefit the client.

The fact is that indexing need not be a terribly labor-intensive activity. There is work to be done in reviewing a client's initial portfolio, crafting a financial plan, and adopting a strategy, but from then on it can involve fairly low maintenance. I say "can" because there is value to heavy education and interaction by the advisors in crafting a sophisticated indexing portfolio that very accurately fits the investor's profile and is closely monitored for rebalancing opportunities and tax harvesting. However, how likely is it that this will lead to outsized returns, after fees for these services are paid? Not terribly likely, in my view. There has never been a time when there were more ways to avoid egregious Wall Street fees and unnecessary services.

CHAPTER 4

Filtering Out the Noise

"One can't say that figures lie. But figures, as used in financial arguments, seem to have the bad habit of expressing a small part of the truth forcibly, and neglecting the other part, as do some people we know."

—Fred Schwed, Jr.[1]

Although companies listed in financial markets produce actual tangible goods and services, trading of their stocks is actually the commerce of information. Whether it is supposedly hot stock tips or thoughtful commentary on buy-and-hold strategies, time-sensitive information is what moves the markets, just as it should.

The crush of short-term financial information is utterly overwhelming. What company was up highest today? Who announced an earnings surprise? What happened to each and every equity in my portfolio? These meaningless questions are answered daily through every available media channel. In most cases investors didn't know such trivia was of use until a newscaster convinces them otherwise.

This financial avalanche of trivia is noise. It seeps into the unwary investor's psyche like earwax. After a certain point it is impossible to hear anything coherent. No indexer can operate effectively without filtering out market noise. Otherwise, it is impossible to focus on long-term objectives, consider important debates, and accomplish prudent maintenance of portfolios. Investors should examine with a critical eye the flow of financial media information available to them and choose what to filter out.

Information regarding individual companies and fund manager strategies should be ignored in favor of high-quality journalism and education that assists critical areas for indexing such as asset allocation, general economic trends, and risk assessment. First an indexer must shut out the part of the financial media that deals with individual company activity. Of course, every individual company in some way affects the larger market, and sometimes a company's success or problems can help shine light on an issue relevant to many other firms. Otherwise, it is useless or sometimes misleading information to the newcomer to investing, and indexers don't believe in picking stocks. Indeed, experienced indexers tend to filter out such information heavily, sifting only for very broad patterns. The ability to filter out individual company information will save an enormous amount of time.

Of course, investors benefit from a basic knowledge of events affecting major firms such as the Microsoft antitrust litigation or the bankruptcy of Enron. Equally, a small sampling of reports of smaller companies may be useful. Anything more should be viewed as entertainment—not harmful, unless confused by real knowledge of relevant information.

Who cares if a company or the market went up or down today? It does affect people's lives, of course, but what can be done about it by the individual investor? On average, absolutely nothing. Financial information is so impossibly detailed and contradictory that investors can't expect to make much sense of it. Earnings reports or articles on individual company events are especially to be filtered out. Stock analysts and professional traders can't even seem to capitalize on it (legally, that is). How is an individual investor going to manage that?

Yes, the detailed reporting of earnings surprises, analysts' consensus, and other company events is essential to the active investor. Luckily, not everyone has to be one. In place of reading all the latest raw earnings reports, the astute indexer saves time to devote to thoughtful analysis of classes of investment assets, general economic trends, taxation, and other relevant issues. Many active investors spend a shocking amount of time on market minutiae. If they worked for salary instead during that time, they would have an impressive amount more to invest. Unfortunately, they spent it watching some financial noisemaker.

Any article that gives an investor insight into risks of asset classes is especially useful. A small number of reports will suffice in helping to learn about differences between actual index investing products and brands. In short, curious investors should take a view of the forest, not the trees, as they learn. Why is it that so much of the financial media cranks out regular streams of "financial noise," whereas reports more appropriate to the average investor are not emphasized? Most financial journalists have all the same problems that Wall Street professionals do and a few extras thrown in. They may fear offending the active management crowd who provide the overwhelming majority of their advertising, so they are often biased, especially upper management.

More importantly, they often are simply inadequately versed in the underlying principles of investment and economics. Even in cases in which a particular journalist is discerning and educated in finance, their editors and producers tend to splash racy headlines suggesting questionable courses of action. Readers often don't read every article, but they will glance at every headline. A short review of the various types of financial media finds rather little outright corruption. There is, however, plenty of sloppiness and lack of interest that leaves media irrelevant and antithetical to the investor's interests.

TELEVISION

Television journalism is largely inoffensive but almost utterly useless to the indexer. The medium simply does not lend itself well to the examination of facts and figures or to the explanation of key long-term investing concepts. It is cursed in this case with the ability to depict immediate events and its inability to communicate the essence of long-term trends. Every viewer has to follow the story at the same pace, which can make the same story annoyingly slow for knowledgeable investors and bewilderingly fast for the novice. Television's best role is to provide interviews with leading thinkers and to summarize major events, such as investigations into the Enron affair.

NEWSPAPERS

Newspapers provide sober, dispassionate articles yet have difficulty covering investment finance as well as they do fast-breaking local news and political issues. Their focus is on breaking news, and most breaking news is essentially market noise. They can provide excellent coverage of an individual company, but how is this translated into greater returns?

Another problem is the newspapers' talent pool. Their writers are often excellent, but few have sufficient financial or mathematical background to feel comfortable reducing complex financial issues to simpler terms for average investors. In one reputable metropolitan daily, I took an informal survey of the 30 or so editors and writers and found no one with serious formal education in finance, statistics, or calculus. They were nearly all history, English, or other humanities students.

Even a newspaper as deep in talent as the *Los Angeles Times* could not see the flaws of the investment strategy of Robert Citron, treasurer for Orange County during the early 1990s. It endorsed him above an opponent who publicly revealed that Citron was buying risky derivatives in a bid to jack up bond returns. "Citron, the incumbent, has been getting a bum rap from the challenger [John Moorlach]," wrote the *Los Angeles Times* during its endorsement of Citron. Eventually, the derivatives drove Orange County into bankruptcy. Sure, Citron had a proven superior track record. But at what risk? The newspaper could not understand the need for appropriate balance of risk and return.

Of course, there are several eminent financial newspapers and news magazines and many strong regional business magazines. *Barron's* is comprehensive and hard-hitting, but somewhat irrelevant to the indexer because of its fairly heavy focus on active stock picking. Its lead columnist, Alan Abelson, is an amusing and skeptical watcher of trends of human financial folly who offers commonsense analysis. Indexers should read him when they can.

The Wall Street Journal is thorough, timely, and accurate, but it too contains a minority of content articles of general economic trends that are useful to the indexer. The indexer seeks only articles featuring opinions of business leaders and economists regarding trends that can offer insight into risks and opportunities for different asset classes. Commentary by staff and outsiders is particularly engaging and stimulating. *The Journal* has an excellent columnist in Jonathan Clements, who examines personal financial planning and investment issues with a relaxed and evenhanded manner. His articles side with most core indexing precepts.

Even *The Journal* has its share of sloppy, uncritical journalism that tends to shield the active crowd. My favorite example is the casual manner in which it reports on its dartboard contest, which was called to a halt in 2002 after 14 years. Started in 1988, the contest pits four stock professionals against four reporters. The professionals select one stock they think will do well over the next six months, while the journalists pitch darts against stock market listings pinned to a wall in the Journal's newsroom. Over 10 years there have been 142 six-month runs. The contest, curiously, was started in response to the growing community of indexers and specifically to test in an open way the random walk theory popularized so well by Burton Malkiel's book *A Random Walk Down Wall Street.*[2]

At first glance, the professionals handily beat the darts, racking up an average 10.2% investment gain versus a modest 3.5% gain for the darts. The Dow Industrials, meanwhile, showed an average gain of 5.6%. The pros beat the darts 87 to 55 and beat the Dow 76 to 66 during the 142 runs. *The Journal's* on-line description of the contest and farewell article in its print version treat the contest as entertaining but also stress that the pros handily beat the dart-throwers and the Dow Jones Industrials Average fair and square.

But did they? Bing Liang, an assistant professor at Case Western Reserve University, looked more closely at the claims and found major problems, one of them quite troubling. It is inconceivable that *The Journal* would not be aware of the Liang study, but no mention was made of it in two articles by *The Journal* on its contest.

The first problem was that darts on average landed on very different stocks than those picked by the pros, and certainly the Dow Industrials bear no relation to the pros' picks. Liang's review of the pros' picks shows they were clearly smaller, riskier stocks than the dart throwers' stocks and definitely much riskier on average than the Dow Industrials. One would expect risky assets to deliver higher returns, so one would expect the pros to win on that basis alone: thus any comparison between the two is an apples-to-oranges comparison. It is possible to even the comparison by adjusting for risk, and that is what Liang did. According to him, "Pros tend to pick stocks with low dividend yield, high systematic risk, and superior past six-month returns." Once he adjusted for risk, he found the pros actually underperformed both the Dow and the darts. Because the contest failed to account for dividend yield, the darts' raw returns were penalized heavily since they tended to carry high dividends.

Next, the randomness of the darts appears in question. According to Liang, "It is surprising that among the 201 dartboard stocks there are 5 stocks which have been hit twice. Remember that these 201 stocks are randomly chosen from about 8000 stocks in *The Wall Street Journal.* The chance of 5 re-appearances should be extremely low. This, together with the large number of financial stocks, raises questions about the random-ness of the dartboard stocks."[3] *The Journal* was literally tacked onto a wall where darts could be thrown at it.

Most troubling by far was "the announcement effect." During the two days before each column appeared announcing new picks by the pros, these stocks would jump an average of 5% if the professional has been in the con-test more than one round. This enormous jump is far more than can be expected by normal appreciation. A stock climbing that high every two days would appreciate over 900% per year! Clearly, someone was getting wind of the anticipated pick and jumping in front of the line, on a regular basis. Then, on the first two days following the announcement the stock contin-ues to gain another 3.5% as investors pile on to ride the momentum.

Unfortunately, gains after an announcement are nearly all given back within a month as investors who got wind of the article prior to publica-tion cash out. The result of not having access to "insider trading" is that actual investors cannot hope to equal the returns obtained by the pros. It could literally be illegal for the stock-picking pro to recommend his or her clients buy because of the impending article, but no one has ever been or is likely to be prosecuted.

The study summed it all up this way: "Overall, pros can neither out-perform the darts nor the market. By examining the pre- and post-contest periods, we find that pros follow relative strength strategies to choose past winners, but the stock prices of these winners tend to be reversed later on. We also document a two-day announcement effect for the pros' stocks, which is complicated by experts' reputation and stock sizes. Our study supports the price pressure hypothesis: abnormal returns and trading vol-umes following the announcement date are driven by noise trading from naïve investors. The seeming "superior" performance of experts' stocks can be explained by the sample size, the announcement effect, the risk factor, and the missing dividend yields."[4]

The Wall Street Journal claims it had strict controls on information leaks regarding the contest. What is clear is that *someone,* probably the pros themselves, was releasing information in an unethical manner, and *The Wall Street Journal* set the stage for this charade each month. The contest resembled the stock-hyping efforts so often reported by *The Journal*. Analysts, company managers and money managers all are tempted to praise stocks when it benefits their firm, but there are limits on how and what they can say.

The Journal certainly has the right to run any contest it cares to, but as a reputable media outlet it has the additional duty of explaining the above facts to its readers, both to help them fairly evaluate the contest and to caution them about using it as an investment tool. Neither in its on-line column about the contest nor in its farewell article did *The Journal* mention the Liang study.

Another example of a strong newspaper showing weak financial reporting was *The New York Times'* use of Mark Hulbert as regular commentator on mutual fund performance. Hulbert's dubious specialty is to track the (typically poor) performance of stock-picking and market-timing newsletters, probably the most amateurish and derided source of financial information and advice available. His unsurprising conclusions are that newsletters on average are a poor tool to time the markets, and indeed that no newsletter has shown sustained predictive powers. This is like a columnist whose specialty was reviewing the *National Enquirer* and other scandal sheet tabloids for accuracy. We are happy to know that someone is chasing this information down, we're just glad we don't have to do it!

One rare article concerning efficient markets that caught our eye appeared in *The Times* on August 15, 2000. Entitled "Dot-Com Makes a Company Smell Sweet," Hulbert commented on a study by Raghavendra Rau and Michael J. Cooper, two assistant professors at Purdue University. In search of market inefficiencies, the study examined patterns of reckless speculation in Internet initial public offerings during the height of the stock bubble in the late 1990s.

The following statement in the article startled me: "Accepting the [Efficient Market] hypothesis means accepting that all money managers' attempts to beat the markets are doomed," wrote Hulbert. We assumed this sloppy statement was meant figuratively, not literally. No one in either active or indexing camps would claim that *all* money managers will fail to beat the market. The issue is whether *on average* the managers will fail, all else being equal. Unfortunately, unsuspecting investors may take him literally.

What further piqued my curiosity was Hulbert's claim that Rau and Cooper had poked holes in the efficient market theory. "A new academic study may finally put to rest the notion, once widely held, that the financial markets efficiently price securites, all the time." Once again, Hulbert is not clear on the theory itself. Very few economists have argued that all information is priced into stocks, but rather that most public information generally is. The inference seemed to be that inefficiencies could be identified by clever professional investors. At IndexFunds.com we try to investigate such claims. It's of special interest to indexers, as we shall see in Chapter 6, because important theories of competition congregate around it. It's generally a fruitless activity, but a sense of humor and a perverse fascination for the subject makes us do it. I telephoned Prof. Rau, one of the co-authors. He essentially contradicted all of Hulbert's claims and insinuations.

Yes, the study of dot-com mania may have uncovered some degree of inefficiency, he said. No, it was not possible to say for sure. No, there was no obvious way to predict the onset of that inefficiency. No, it did not seem as though it could be easily exploited without risk. It was likely to short-lived. To quote him: "Can we predict where markets might be inefficient? One problem is that we do not have a theoretical model of inefficiency—what we have is a bunch of anomalies which may indicate market inefficiency. So prediction is almost impossible. In addition, alternative explanations have been suggested for these anomalies and so we have a current on-going argument as to what these results really mean. The dot-com paper evidence is evidence against market efficiency, but again we cannot conclusively say that markets are inefficient on the basis of these results."

It's a problem when the main source for an article completely refutes the article's major thesis. In general, my impression is that standards for reporting and fact checking are not quite as strong in personal finance as they are in other parts of most media. Personal finance will affect readers concretely more than political intrigue, and readers have more power to change their own financial world more than their political representation. Still newspapers are far more focused on unearthing the latest Watergate than helping readers grow wealthy.

MAGAZINES

Mildly disappointing are financial magazines. Here is the perfect medium for educating indexers. Its infrequent publication dates and longer articles could be used to address major issues of long-term wealth creation. Instead, a shocking number scream for investors to buy this or that hot mutual fund. They help to foster a juvenile approach to investing and greedy attitudes, as evidenced by the endless parade of top ten stock and fund lists to make investors rich now.

SmartMoney has been a favorite because it so tirelessly exposes the tricks used to separate investors from their money. It was a rare advocate for the average investor. But its cover articles now trumpet hot stocks of the month. Apparently its philosophy has changed. Also, *Mutual Funds Magazine* is full of thoughtful, serious commentary, as is *Online Investor.* None of these pound home the obvious dangers of high fees and turnover as much as I would like to see, but the fact is that many of their readers simply don't care. The general business magazines such as *Forbes, Fortune,* and *BusinessWeek* also educate the indexer on general business trends and skim over individual company trivia.

There are many more magazines at the more dangerous end of the spectrum. With few exceptions, they are to be avoided. Someday perhaps a true indexer's magazine will come to fruition.

BOOKS

Books are also an excellent medium for the long-term investor, but they fall on both ends of the quality spectrum. A substantial number of fine books educate and instruct the investor in indexing and passive investing methodologies. Many discuss the various points of strategy. Most books, however, hype foolish day-trading activity to amateurs with too much time on their hands.

If stockbrokers were doing such a great job, they wouldn't be so much richer than their clients! In 1940 a Princeton dropout and short-lived stockbroker named Fred Schwed, Jr., wrote one of the earliest and funniest books on Wall Street, *Where Are the Customers' Yachts?* The characters on Wall Street and their motivations don't seem to have changed a bit. It could have been written today. More should.

According to Schwed, "Books about Wall Street fall into two categories which may respectively be called the admiring, or the "Oh, my!" School, and the vindictive, or "Turn the Rascals Out" School. Needless to say, the former were all written formerly, and the latter, latterly, the dividing line being around October, 1929. Neither school assays more than a few pounds of open-mindedness to the ton, and that noble occupation, Deep Thinking, continues to be, as ever, mostly second guessing."

RESEARCH GROUPS

Millions of investors try to make sense of it all by relying on independent third-party rating outfits such as Morningstar. This and other research groups form an indispensable part of the financial media today. Morningstar sells a wealth of useful information regarding mutual funds to professionals and researchers, but its star system is not its proudest achievement. This firm's star rating system give from one to five stars to mutual funds according to how well they have done in past years. The problem is that the stars are virtually useless, if not downright misleading.

Although Morningstar warns in the small print that the star system is not to be taken as a predictor of future performance, that's exactly how fund groups promote it. They splash enormous advertisements in financial magazines hyping their five-star-rated funds, and investors respond by surging into these funds, ignoring even three- and four-star rated funds.

To begin with, grade inflation with the star system is more rampant than at Harvard University. In 2002 approximately one-third of mutual funds were earning top grades of four or five stars.[5] Because the actual returns were so poor in 2001, fund advertisements conveniently removed returns and placed greater emphasis on stars, which track performance relative to peers. Readers were shielded from the essential knowledge that these funds can go down in value.

One unique study that is germane to the individual investor is Stanford University Professor William Sharpe's examination of the Morningstar fund rating system.

In 1998 Sharpe examined the predictive behavior of these ratings in his study "Morningstar's Risk-adjusted Ratings." One would expect five-star-rated funds would continue to perform well, and one-star funds would continue to bomb, right? Unfortunately, there is very little correlation between past and future performance.

Funds with modest ratings were truly scattered in their subsequent returns. There was no discernible trend among them. The worst laggards continue to trail more commonly than not, which isn't much help to individual investors but does beg the question of how. It turns out that in the mutual fund cellar is a heavy concentration of funds with even higher fees than their counterparts. They are literally dragged down by the greed of their managers.

These conclusions do not even take into account transaction costs and taxes paid when switching from hot fund to hot fund (since they rarely stay on top year to year). Furthermore, Morningstar's star system weights heavily towards sectors that are hot: so-so performing funds in hot sectors tend to be rated higher than top performing funds in so-so performing sectors.

Writes Sharpe: "Star risk-adjusted ratings summarize both the performance of the domain in which a fund operates and the performance of the fund relative to others in its domain. Selection of funds with high star risk-adjusted ratings is far more likely to result in the choice of funds in categories with strong recent performance rather than in funds in categories with poor recent performance. In many cases this is likely to be a poor approach to fund selection. There is little evidence that investment in categories that have done well in the last three years is a superior investment strategy."[6]

The hottest 25% of funds had a slightly better than average chance of beating their peers for a year or so, followed by no visible differences. The momentum was not enough to make up for the high fees these funds typically charged, and to capitalize on this trend, the investor would have to hop from hot fund to hot fund fairly quickly, no doubt picking up extra charges along the way. There may have been a small "free lunch," but it had to be eaten fast!

WORLD WIDE WEB

Let me reserve my favorite critique for my own current medium, the World Wide Web. Probably no medium has greater potential to empower investors and to help them assess various investing techniques, and yet most investment Web sites are either mired in useless individual stock minutiae or frenetic stock tip sharing between day-traders.

The big sites have plenty of solid and mostly irrelevant information. CBSMarketwatch.com, MotleyFool.com, TheStreet.com, Morningstar.com, and others do an excellent job of following the latest big earnings surprises that either made investors rich or poor that day, as well as general market trends. The articles are well written, delivered in a very timely fashion, and largely irrelevant to the purposes of the buy-and-hold investor. Why should individual investors care which stock had high volume of trading that day unless they are twitchy day-traders? Or even if the entire market went up that day?

Well, twitchy day-trading investors do seem to care, and wherever they go on-line brokerages are sure to follow. They also serve well the buy-and-hold investor with sufficient discipline. By far the dominant sponsors on these and other reputable sites are brokerage firms, who are entirely compensated by the amount of trading that occurs on their sites. They love detailed reporting on market minutiae because it leads to day-traders. When bulletin boards start up, they are generally focused on hot stock tips, charting, and other information appealing to the fast-trigger investor. And so the circle is complete.

The connection between a media focused on day-trading and its advertisers on the Web is most crudely demonstrated in *www.clearsta tion.com,* a stock picker's community site that was purchased in the late 1990s by E*Trade Group, the powerhouse Web brokerage house. This firm does not have many media holdings, and the practice is thankfully rare across the industry.

Apparently in this case it saw a real strategic fit. Upon purchase, E*Trade began pumping huge sums into ClearStation's marketing campaigns in an attempt to grow traffic. Guess who's banner ad sits prominently above most key pages? E*Trade's, of course. Other advertisers are scarce. Where does it say on the site that ClearStation is a wholly owned subsidiary of the brokerage firm? Tucked at the bottom of the "About Us" in small print. Probably only a small proportion of ClearStation visitors are aware of this connection. Everyone can come to their own conclusion, but to me this "content" site looks too much like a media front designed to stimulate trading demand for E*Trade.

This in no way reduces the enormous contribution on-line brokerage firms have made. Perhaps no group of firms has done more in the past decade to empower the individual investor and lower transaction costs. They are to be congratulated and acknowledged as a true friend of the indexer. E*Trade in particular did more than any other to keep quality of service high while driving down costs. Their trading services are top-notch, and I recommend them highly, despite their questionable foray into media.

DISCLAIMER

I freely admit that I have my own axe to grind, which includes benefiting from the inexorable rise in indexing, and I think we are doing a reasonable job of providing independent information at IndexFunds.com. However, our budget is a shoestring compared to the other big Web players. The fact is that the indexing community charges too little to its customers to have much in the way of advertising dollars. We cannot support a constant stream of in-depth articles and studies, much less promote them.

Just as it is liberating for the investor to understand why and how Wall Street professionals must push their high-priced active investment services, it is empowering for the investor to see how the financial media must flood information channels with useless and thoughtless minutiae. The daily assault of financial information no longer causes anxiety or confusion, because the disciplined indexer considers only a manageable, even surprisingly small amount of events and issues. It's like stepping out of a busy street with horns honking and into a quiet café where you can chat with friends on issues of real importance to your life. Your mind is at ease, not irritable, challenged but not overwhelmed.

Thinking about indexing is less of a purely numbers-driven affair once you recognize patterns in the flow of financial information. At the risk of seeming "touchy-feely," I will venture that this harmonizes the use of figures with words to understand the problem and unites left-brain thinking with right-brain thinking. Feeling this balance will help investors attain true comfort with their plan of action.

CHAPTER 5

What Really Smart
Money Thinks

*"I'd compare stock pickers to astrologers, but I don't want
to bad-mouth the astrologers."*

—Eugene Fama, University of Chicago Finance Professor

Financial markets are competitive, or we could all place easy bets
and get rich instantly. *But how competitive are they?* Are they so
competitive that it is a poor wager to spend resources, time, and energy
to try to beat them? Or are there certain clever managers we can identify
in advance who will lead us to riches? This is the crucial debate the novice
indexer must confront, and it is an increasingly important one for the
investment community as a whole. If markets are quite competitive, then
it will be less easy for talented thinkers to shine.

Likewise, playing financial markets clearly benefits from both skill
and luck. But how much is skill and how much of the rest is luck?
Absolute ignorance of investment can be dangerous, but plenty of mod-
erately knowledgeable investors do well, whereas the fancy moves of truly
skilled traders often get them into trouble. Clearly, if you overpay for a
supposedly skilled manager who is merely lucky, you are worse off than
before.

These are called "non-trivial questions" among the deep thinkers. I prefer not to make any quick assumptions about them. If you were to ask someone's opinion on these subjects, you might start with the most intelligent individuals in economics and finance with no conflicts of interest, Nobel laureate economists, for instance. It just happens that virtually no Nobel laureate, indeed, almost no leading independent U.S. economist, has expressed support of Wall Street professionals' claims that they can outperform the average markets on average consistently. The only eminent economists who have examined the issue closely and who have taken a strong stand disagree with Wall Street on its core claims. Eugene Fama, Burton Malkiel, William Sharpe, Paul Samuelson are among the best known, but there are many more.

Probably the best reason to listen to really smart money is that it does not have conflicts of interest. Leading economists not employed by Wall Street generally have tenured professorships, and their salaries do not decline if they offend investment bankers (or even other economists). What do they say? In 1998 Nobel prize winner Paul Samuelson, said: "There are very few people or organizations who have any presumptive edge over a low-cost, no-load set of indices, particularly on a risk corrected basis. People used to say that you're settling for mediocrity. Isn't it interesting that the best brains on Wall Street can't achieve mediocrity?"[1]

Stanford University Professor William Sharpe, who won the Nobel prize in 1990, had the following to say after he personally examined the historical record of mutual fund managers: "While measures of historic variability can be useful for predicting future levels of risk, there is ample evidence that measures of average or cumulative return are at best highly imperfect predictors of expected future return."[2] Past behavior gives almost no clue to future events, even on average, according to Sharpe.

These men are renowned educators who speak plainly to investors on plain issues. They are not ivory tower researchers. Sharpe is also the inventor of the Sharpe ratio that tracks risk-adjusted return, that is, return based on the degree of risk taken on. That's a more useful rating than straight returns, and is covered later in Chapter 18 in which we pick funds.

The list of brilliant, unbiased individuals who discount Wall Street claims for active management is long while the list of those who believe Wall Street is short indeed. Of course, you might ignore the advice of really smart money and take the word of your stockbroker or, worse yet, your friend the amateur stock picker who stays at home and day-trades. They do radiate confidence, and they often are well versed in market trivia and stock-picking jargon. But they are hardly the sort of persons to speak with authority on intricacies of asset allocation, where there is real value added.

Here is a typical Wall Street professional describing a day's trading: "These things seem to pop up at you unexpectedly and then you are saying, 'oh boy.' Nobody knows what is coming next," said Larry Lawler, head of stock trading at Dreyfus Corp., a major mutual fund group, one April morning in 2002 to a *Wall Street Journal* reporter in response to the latest drops in technology stocks.[3] But then again there is nothing very deep to say about any market on any particular day, just as there is nothing very deep to say about today's weather. Financial and meteorological storms come and go, but what greater knowledge does watching them bring us?

The fundamental question is: "How competitive are the markets?" Every time investment professionals speak, you will hear them address this question in some way. If you listen closely, you will invariably hear them agree that markets today are intensely competitive.

If you watch the flow of money, it will give you a clue to where more and more "smart" money is going. The larger and more sophisticated the investors, the more likely they are to index. Estimates from top indexing firms suggest that by 2002 about one quarter of global institutional equity funds such as pension funds were indexed and/or passively managed. On the individual investor side, however, estimates generally hover around 15% in the United States and far less in many other countries. These figures are naturally much larger when they include quiet passive funds that keep transactions way down or "closet index funds" that look a lot like index funds but won't admit to it. However, even if you define indexing as following a clearly defined public list of firms, the large, well-heeled pools of money advised by the cleverest financial minds have made their feelings clear: They are opting out of the financial rat race.

Competition is the watchword for the index investor. No one, absolutely no one, denies that there is competition in the markets today. Whenever it exists in a high degree, the sensible investor will conclude that there will not be any easy pickings. If an investor were to start a gas station, would he or she locate in a small town with two stations already in business or right next to a new superhighway with no stations around for miles? If the investors wanted to get some exercise playing basketball, would they go to an NBA team and audition or would they go to the nearest playground and join a pick-up game?

All around us are examples of where competition restricts our choices, and we react in sensible ways to these restrictions when we understand them. Everyone seems to agree that if there is a free lunch out there, it better be eaten quickly or someone else will get their hands on it! The main point of disagreement is that Wall Street managers all seem to think they are faster than the next. Of course, they seek to earn salaries by joining in that competition and will claim that they are better than the rest, but they will not hesitate to say how hard it is.

How investors interact competitively is a very different question and frankly one of less relevance to beginning investors. Discussions about the finer points of Efficient Market Theory or some other school of thought are as likely to confuse the novice indexers as to assist them. The key word to recall and focus on when the esoteric debates rage is "competition." If the speaker agrees that competition is keen out in the marketplace, then common sense suggests one should avoid it.

Benjamin Graham, another eminent investment thinker who supported key tenets of indexing, is considered the father of modern analysis of publicly traded companies. Although the concept of indexing did not exist remotely then in the way we know it now, he vigorously promoted a sensible approach to investing that has many parallels. According to Graham, in a bull market, huge returns can be posted using unorthodox and unsound methods. "Such results in themselves may indicate only that the fund managers are taking undue speculative risks, and getting away with same for the time being."[4]

History tells us that "performance funds" that promise huge returns are almost always run by young men whose only financial experience is limited to a continuous bull market, he said. These young men almost always are interested in the short-term fluctuations in stock prices (momentum). Their real talent is in exploiting the speculative furor that sweeps over a greedy public, according to Graham.

Financial "miracles" are usually the result of manipulation, misleading corporate reporting (see Enron), shaky capitalization structures, and fraud.

Graham believed that although new laws are enacted to curb speculation after a bubble, in reality it's impossible to fully extinguish the urge to speculate by fund managers themselves! "All financial experience up to now indicates that large funds, soundly managed, can produce at best only slightly better than average results over the years. If they are unsoundly managed they can produce spectacular, but largely illusory, profits for a while, followed inevitably by calamitous losses."[5]

For unbiased studies that compare actively managed funds to index benchmarks, the primary source is academia. University economists are relatively unbiased, arguably the brightest in their field, and schooled in the scientific method, not rhetorical flourishes. They may embrace incompatible theories of how the markets work, they may use elaborate formulas and technical jargon, and they may find temporary exceptions.

But when it comes around to asking whether the average investor is likely to beat the market, their answers are pretty much the same: Markets are competitive, and it is unlikely that the individual investor is going to beat them, whether by hiring a star mutual fund manager or by stock picking on their own. Why do you think that you will have access to information others won't have: Why do you think your manager will be able to conceal his stock picks for long?

Many thinkers have engaged in long debates on exactly how the market goes about being competitive. These are fascinating and complex debates about the fundamental nature of how human beings interact in the giant board game called financial speculation. The bottom line is that competition in markets is very tough, and if indeed it is tough to beat the market, then to the beginning investor it really doesn't matter so much why.

On the discussion boards of IndexFunds.com we see lots of beginning investors get hung up on advanced economic theory. About half the time it is clear they lack the financial background to truly grasp the theory they are criticizing. The rest of the time they make excellent points on theory but don't make a clear connection between theory and their own portfolio.

They enjoy the intellectual banter, but does their retirement fund benefit from it? The type of assets picked explains almost all of the returns on Wall Street. Stock picking, whether good, bad or indifferent, explains very little of the return. So why not put most of your time into choosing asset classes wisely, and very little or even none into stock picking?

What did legendary stock analyst Benjamin Graham think of trying to pick star managers? The "trick" is to find funds that will outperform in the future and obtain "the most capable management without paying any special premium [in terms of expense ratio] for it against the other funds." In other words, he wasn't against finding managers who appear capable, he just didn't feel it was worth paying extra for them! It begs the question, Why should anyone pay the extra premium for *any* managed fund when an index fund will do just fine?

Whenever competition wanes, the subtle investors concede that the market average is no longer the obvious choice. Investors are at a crossroads: They may engage in active picking of the financial instruments where there is so little competition, or they may ignore that asset class entirely.

Very small company (micro-cap) stocks and mid-sized corporate bonds are a good example. Clever financial analysts in this arena can operate without nearly as much competition as in the larger company arena. Gems can be identified early on without others jumping in immediately. The problem is that often these analysts must do a great deal of extra leg work to make up for the lack of other analysts and of media reports from which to glean information. Consequently, investors pay a great deal for this advice and must depend upon a relatively thin layer of analysis. Do they really have confidence in the analyst or not? Clearly, even if the answer is yes, listening to just one person is more of a gamble. It is hard for investors to know whether the analyst is forthright or is withholding their full opinion out of fear of losing investment banking business for their firm.

Clearly the risk of this asset class must be viewed as greater purely from the point of view of the information flow. It is simply very hard to know with so very little information.

CHAPTER 6

In Theory, at Least

*With all that is known about the poor results of active stock
picking, why do so many investors still buy high-cost
mutual funds and churn their stock portfolios? The answer
is simple: because they are told to do so, every day, explicitly
or implicitly, by the financial media and their advertisers.*

—Gregory Baer and Gary Gensler
The Great Mutual Fund Trap, Broadway, 2002.

Just about every plausible theory of the markets today suggests that
stiff competition makes it tough to beat the publicly traded stock
market without taking on extra risk. It should be difficult to beat markets,
regardless of the theory you pick. You don't really need a degree in finance
to know how managers did as a group against the averages. Simple algebra
does it for us. It goes like this:

1. Average return of all funds after fees = average return before
   fees – fees, and since all funds can

2. Average index fund = average return before fees – very low fees,
   and

3. Average active fund = average return before fees – high fees and
   since high fees exceed low fees,

4. Net return of average index fund > net return of average active fund

Any single manager can beat low-cost indexes, but by mathematical definition they must fail as a group. If a manager is taking out high fees, they had better be extra good. Another basic and relevant theory is that of random distribution of natural phenomena, better known as luck.

When the weather turns hot during a particular season, certain plants win out and others lose. Insect species that fared poorly last year in the cold now multiply, while their cold-weather adversaries fade away. It just so happens that most activity in nature falls into what looks like a bell-shaped curve when plotted on a piece of paper. Outliers on either side of the curve are less common. They are the lucky and the unlucky. The further out to either side you go, the less you should expect to see. But you should always expect to see some at the very outer edges (see Figure 6.1). Stock market returns are no different. The returns fall into neat bell-shaped curves. They certainly look like random natural phenomena.

A linchpin concept that crosses theoretical boundaries is that asset class selection is far more important that stock picking in explaining

FIGURE 6.1   DISTRIBUTION OF RETURNS OF 1305 LARGE-BLEND FUNDS

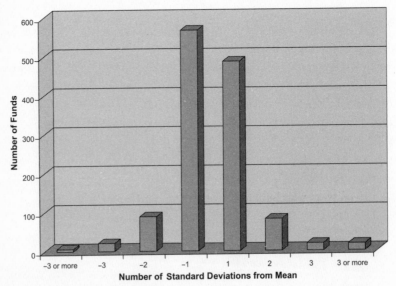

SOURCE: Morningstar data as of 4/30/2002

portfolio performance. This was first pointed out in the study "Determinants of Portfolio Performance" study by Gary Brinson and colleagues and published in the *Financial Analysts Journal* in 1986. Reviewed and confirmed in general terms over time by other economists, it found that approximately 94% of a money manager's returns could be explained, for better or for worse, by the selection of the class of asset. Of course, it mattered what individual stocks were picked, but not nearly as much. The portfolio's fate was determined almost exclusively by the set of asset classes for the long run. Market timing explained a mere 2% of the returns, while stock selection explained only 4%. The study suggests that if a money manager seems impressive, it will not be because of purported stock-picking abilities but rather because of the ability to pick general asset classes cleverly.

Market timing, or the ability to step in and out of major asset classes deftly, is a tempting strategy for the indexer. Especially if you own an exchange-traded fund, it is quite easy to buy and sell one's fund at regular intervals. Unfortunately, every study of market timing has shown market timing to fail. Why? Markets generally drift upward, so stepping out of the market just because it seems fully valued exposes one to missing a bull ride. In addition a majority of price climbs occur during just a few dozen trading days each year.

On the defensive side, trying to avoid market downturns is a tricky affair. In 1999 and 2000 when everyone was transfixed by high Internet company valuations, a much larger wave of overvaluation snuck up on the market: telecommunications. The amount of money lost in telecom stocks has been estimated to be 10 times that which was lost on Internet stocks. Probably what caught most investors off guard was the degree to which it came from seemingly stable and well-run telephone companies such as AT&T and WorldCom. So the question also becomes: What makes you think you can identify the more surprising downturn, and not just the fairly obvious bubble?

The phenomenal importance of asset class selection comes from the fact that members of a class of assets or market sector move together in price. Sure, some auto manufacturers may do better in a given year than others, but if people just aren't buying cars, every company suffers. If consumers are in the mood, then even the auto maker with lemons will get some lift. Thus, managers who own lots of health stocks just as they rise as a group do not succeed primarily by identifying promising individual companies but rather by identifying a promising industrial sector. If they had chosen other members of the group, they also would have done well. Not the same, of course, but well enough.

Another rather straightforward concept with voluminous evidence from many fields of study is called reversion to the mean. Simply put, stocks and market sectors that enjoyed unusually high returns in the past are more likely to revert to mean, or average returns, or what goes up fast is not likely to keep going up so fast. Used extensively in scientific research such as population studies, reversion to the mean is so naturally associated with the rhythms of natural phenomena that it is considered a statistical rule of thumb in many fields. It has every bit as much meaning in investments, which is not so surprising if one considers that humans are at the center of all financial decisions.

This is not at all the same as saying, "What goes up must go down," but rather that what went up at a high rate is bound to slow down to a typical rate. Thus, a stock that went from $100 to $120 for a 20% return must reach $144, $172, and $207 in successive years to continue its pace. The sheer weight of compounding interest makes this increasingly difficult to do. The longer the string of outsized success, the more unlikely its continuation. Reversion to the mean has been proven again and again in studies of financial markets. It is particularly relevant to the novice investor, because it is so easy to understand and can be applied so effectively to protect against risky speculation. It is entirely in harmony with the standard manner of maintaining index portfolios to their original target through the practice of rebalancing, which we shall examine later in Chapter 19.

What reversion to the mean cannot assist in is prediction strategies such as market timing. It is too blunt an instrument. Peter Bernstein, who examined risk throughout history in his book *Against the Gods,* sums up the difficulty of using reversion, or regression as he calls it, as a predictive guide to investing: "There are three reasons why regression to the mean can be such a frustrating guide to decision-making. First, it sometimes proceeds at so slow a pace that a shock will disrupt the process. Second, the regression may be so strong that matters do not come to rest once they reach the mean. Rather they fluctuate around the mean, with repeated, irregular deviations on either side. Finally, the mean itself may be unstable, so that yesterday's normality may be supplanted today by a new normality that we know nothing about."[1]

We echo the majority opinion among index practitioners that reversion to the mean is a valuable concept to support long-term buy-and-hold strategies, rebalancing, and occasional side stepping of clearly overpriced asset classes.

On a rare occasion you will find IndexFunds.com defending active investing, and one of them is the issue of "cash drag." Cash drag refers to a drop in overall returns from the practice by active mutual funds of keeping a small percentage of assets in cash, usually about 2% to 5%, in order to cushion against investor withdrawals. In contrast, index funds keep almost no cash on hand.

Actively managed funds have a practical problem. As stock pickers, they concentrate their holdings on a relatively small number of companies, and the purchase and sale of those stocks in large blocks tends to impact the price far more than a widely diversified index fund with 5 to 100 times as many holdings (unless the active fund is a closet index fund). Even upon small dips, investors tend to pull out their money in a hurry. Money managers hate this! They prefer to buy low and sell high, and rightly so. When they pick well, their concentrated positions benefit them; when they pick poorly, their concentrated positions hurt them equally. Unfortunately, because of investor psychology inflows tend to come in steadily and leave in a rush, so as an operational matter money managers are at a disadvantage. Active funds are forced in practice to keep a cushion of cash. Those are the rules of the game they play. Active funds on average will lag the benchmark they are targeting by a few percentage points simply from holding a bit more cash. This is cash drag.

Why do I think this is not on its face an advantage, all else being equal, for index funds? Because investors always can hike the amount allocated to an active fund by the amount of cash kept in that fund. If a fund generally keeps 4% in cash and investors had intended to allocate 70% of their portfolio for stocks, they can simply allocate 74% to the active fund in question to achieve the desired overall allocation. It should be noted that the typical active fund investor still pays a hefty annual fee on the portion kept in cash as well as the portion kept in stocks, so all else is not exactly equal.

COMPETITION AND EFFICIENCY

Leading early twentieth-century economist John Maynard Keynes greatly advanced understanding of the mechanisms of business activity, especially in relation to capital. However, he remained skeptical about any system that could predict changes in economic activity. "Animal spirits" or inexplicable mood swings among the populace and investors wereas detailed an explanation for changes as he was willing to offer.

Then, during the 1960s and 1970s an economic theory concerning competition took hold that remains dominant among academicians. It is called the Efficient Market Theory. It says that markets are fairly priced when business information is spread out to investors who incorporate it into their decisions. This information is incorporated into decisions so that investors collectively settle on prices that balance the myriad of factors and influences present at that moment. The process happens continuously in real time.

Some see the theory as relevant to the active versus index debate because it is felt by many that if markets are efficient, excess profits will not be gained easily. Many view the theory as a useful but not comprehensive system of thought, much like Newtonian physics. Others debate its logic entirely and call it wrong-spirited, but even most of its critics concede that the market is quite competitive. Virtually everyone agrees that even if there are market inefficiencies, it does not mean that they are consistently exploitable. These opportunities come and go in unpredictable ways, then mutate, and soon enough vanish. Latecomers infrequently ride the wave fully. Early adopters may be skilled (rather than lucky), but how is an outsider (the investor judging the money manager) to know until the track record is established? By that time, it is often too late. The beginning indexer is encouraged not to get caught up in lengthy debate over this theory.

Discussion of Efficient Market Theory can get quite complicated, but the following short primer should be sufficient: Investors are "rational," that is to say self-interested, and they buy and sell in a way they think will increase their wealth. Of course, they are not always right, and certainly they can be irrational in the sense of exuberant or panic-stricken, but they are always rational in the sense of self-interest. They always act in the belief that they are improving their financial situation.

At IndexFunds.com we encounter a surprising number of persons who refuse to adopt the special use of "rational" and believe this allows them to refute the entire theory. This is a little like saying that gravity is a serious state of mind and not a physical concept and that therefore objects cannot drop. I suggest that they substitute the word "self-interested."

Thus, if enough investors turn their attention to information concerning a stock or bond, goes the theory, the competition to buy as low as possible and to sell as high as possible (since everyone is self-interested) inevitably leads to "efficiency." As a result, information and expectations gathered by millions of analysts and traders will be reflected by stock prices. It is unlikely that additional research into this information will result in higher profits.

Efficiency has three flavors, called the weak, semistrong, and strong versions. The weak version is the easiest to prove. It says that past securities prices are disseminated so widely and quickly that they cannot be exploited consistently to gain an edge in the marketplace. For instance, virtually anyone can follow securities prices during trading, and reams of past trades can be downloaded for examination. If there was a consistent trend that could be counted on, traders would flock to exploit it and take all the profits available, thus removing the trend.

It turns out, according to a study of large-cap U.S. stocks by Professor Richard Roll at UCLA, that while there may be significant imbalances at the market opening between sell orders and buy orders for a stock, day-to-day there is no discernible trend that can be exploited to beat the long-term return.[2] The market essentially goes from inefficient to efficient, at least as far as publicly available prices are concerned, every day during market trading. How long does it take for the market to go from inefficient to weak-form efficient? About 30 minutes, it turns out.

The popularity of the Efficient Market Theory among economists, who love to conduct studies and publish papers, is partly due to its ability to be proven or disputed with actual data. The Roll study is one of hundreds. The next form of efficiency, semistrong, states that press releases, analysts' reports, and other less visible but nonetheless public types of information make their way into prices in such a way that trading on them gives no discernible edge. Most students of economics agree with this.

Finally, the strong form of efficiency states that all information, including insider or management information whether it is traded legally or illegally, is priced into the market quickly and accurately. There is considerably more skepticism about this assertion. There should be increasing consensus on the line of actual efficiency in the market, as plenty of researchers are scouring the data for clear signs of inefficiency. Purdue's Raghavendra Rau is one who is confident that inefficiencies exist and more will be found. This doesn't mean he believes that they are common or that they can be exploited with ease by massive numbers of investors: "... I believe that the market will always tend towards efficiency. Research gets published. After a paper on the positive long-run performance of firms announcing share repurchases, buyback funds were set up to take advantage of exactly this phenomenon, thus driving the potential returns towards zero."[3]

CRITICS OF EFFICIENT MARKETS

One particularly intriguing critique of the Efficient Market Theory has been developed by Professor Richard Haugen of UCLA. He raises the dominant anomaly among stocks: Why do value stocks outperform growth stocks fairly reliably and offer apparently lower risk? This is not an anecdotal phenomenon but rather based on groundbreaking research by Eugene Fama and Kenneth French when they were at the University of Chicago and MIT, respectively. Haugen notes that value stocks perennially outperform their growth cousins, and he criticizes the internal logic of the Efficient Market Theory because of the outsized performance of a class of large-company U.S. stocks he calls Super Stocks. In short, they are value stocks that have shown earnings growth but as yet not much appreciation in their stock price. The market hasn't taken them seriously, but after a quarter or two of strong performance it does with a vengeance.

This is actually a wonderful example of reversion to the mean. As Haugen points out in his book, *The New Finance: The Case Against Efficient Markets*, winners growing fast tend to slow down and losers growing slowly tend to speed up (on average, that is). Such stocks have shown excellent performance in recent decades, and according to him that couldn't be if the markets were efficient. Still, he doesn't think this means investors need an active manager. They can simply buy from his list of Super Stocks, which is essentially an index. It is a list based on more complex criteria than size of company or price-to-earnings (p/e) ratios, but not an attempt to pick stocks based on judgement. You needn't be an Efficient Market Theory enthusiast to be an indexer. All you have to do is have a clever view on asset allocation, which is largely what Haugen's theory espouses.[4]

How can this inefficiency occur? Partly because institutional money managers are desperate to achieve short-term profits (remember the marketing treadmill?), and they have no interest in keeping risk down. Curiously, all they care about is keeping up with their respective benchmarks, typically the S&P 500. They are not eager to lower volatility, because no one follows those numbers. Everyone is watching CNN to see how the S&P did that afternoon! Clearly, the argument is intriguing, and it explains a lot. The fetish for the S&P 500 is essentially tied to consumer ignorance, or perhaps I should say lack of education. Many investors associate indexing only with the S&P 500.

Of course, these purportedly easy profits would shrink if more investors take his relatively public advice and drive up Super Stock prices. Haugen argues that this is not likely soon because of the willingness of mutual fund managers to take on high risks to beat their benchmarks. Ultimately, no one in economics argues hard against the pervasive presence of competition. If it were easy to pick winning stocks, they would be counting their millions in a villa on their own island.

The problem with *any* scheme to beat the market based on historical returns is that you often can't be sure the trend it is built on wasn't simply a random occurrence. With so many possible periods to choose from and so many possible stock features (p/e ratios, size, etc.), it is virtually a certainty that some remarkable string of successes will show up in a study of the past. Statistics can even pinpoint with relative precision how likely such anomalies are to exist. The answer is that it is quite likely, given so many possible scenarios.

Attempting to find an unusual historical trend is called *data mining*. This is the practice of sifting through every possible period of time for every possible stock feature to find one combination that stands out. To put it mildly, it is viewed with skepticism by serious researchers. The identification of such a trend doesn't mean it is very likely to continue, and it certainly doesn't mean it would have been very easy to predict PRIOR to the trend. The length of a trend is not necessarily any more convincing. Jay Shanken, a finance professor at the University of Rochester's Simon Graduate School of Business Administration, found one investment strategy that consistently lost money for a 27-year period and then promptly made money for the following 27 years.[5]

George Soros, the legendary currency speculator who has taken issue with the Efficient Market Theory, has his own theory of market dynamics called reflexivity: ". . . this (Efficient Market Theory) interpretation of the way financial markets operate is severely distorted. It may seem strange that a patently false theory should gain such widespread acceptance, except for one consideration; that is, that all our theories about social events are distorted in some way or another."[6]

"I operate using a different theory, according to which financial markets cannot possibly discount the future correctly because they do not merely discount the future; they help to shape it. In certain circumstances, financial markets can affect the so-called fundamentals which they are supposed to reflect. When that happens, markets enter into a state of dynamic disequilibrium and behave quite differently from what would be considered normal by the theory of efficient markets. Such boom/bust sequences do not arise very often, but when they do, they can be very disruptive, exactly because they affect the fundamentals of the economy."[7]

Many economists see in his words an unwillingness to agree on common terms. No economist is saying that financial markets discount the future "correctly" in the sense of having a crystal ball that sees into the future. All Efficient Market Theory claims is that information in its imperfect and dispersed form is priced into markets, for better or for worse, and that there is no obvious way to second-guess the markets. In a sense, Soros simply preaches common sense. If reasonable people think a true bubble (and not just fully valued stocks) is looming, perhaps it is time to sidestep it, regardless of how well it is priced on a theoretical level.

In practice, he engages in incredibly risky forms of speculation not investment as most persons understand it. He made his fortune taking huge positions of highly leveraged currency options and other derivatives. It is perfectly conceivable that persons such as he should exist. The smaller the number of speculative forays, the harder it is to identify true skill. The card player who can beat Las Vegas playing over 200 hands of cards over a day's span can be called skilled, but is the same true of a high roller who bets heavily and wins on one or two hands? And indeed that was Soros's practice, according to his longtime associate Victor Niederhoffer: "If he has a chance to make a killing in a market, he is not afraid to put an important proportion of his chips into it. The amount of money he invested in speculation that the British pound would be devalued in 1992 represented a rather staggering proportion of his assets at the time. (I am relying on published accounts on this, as opposed to any knowledge I might have gained.) The result was fame and fortune."[8]

In the late 1990s, however, Soros' currency hedge funds took enormous hits, losing billions of dollars of investor assets. Wanting to make a killing and actually accomplishing it are very different things. Despite Soros' belief in the presence of inefficiencies, he also thinks markets can be very competitive. In an unusual public announcement, he announced a major retrenchment from hedge fund activity based on speculation. The reason? Eager investors had bid up prices for equities to such a degree that the room left for profit was too small and the risks too great. Generally, he wanted out of the game.

A historian of speculation takes a jaundiced view of the Efficient Market Theory in past centuries. Edward Chancellor writes in *Devil Take the Hindmost*, his treatise on speculation through the centuries, that: "Believers in efficient markets claim that speculators help to 'discover' values and that stock prices move randomly because they reflect all information relevant to their value. In the nineteenth-century American market, however, intrinsic values were actually hidden by the operations of speculators. Under such conditions, the outsider could only trust to luck in making an investment decision. This suggests a 'random walk' of a different nature; not the randomness of efficiency where every share price reflects its current inherent value and future changes in price come about only on the receipt of new information, but the randomness of manipulation where a stock might be bulled, beared, trapped, gunned or cornered at the whim of a small clique of operators."[9]

The origins of the "random walk" are amusing. Apparently, the phrase originally appeared in a 1905 article in *Nature* magazine on how one can predict the path of a drunkard staggering through a field. How apt a metaphor for many investors.

COMPLEX SYSTEMS

Another compelling and very different explanation of dynamics is called *complex systems*. It suggests viewing markets as a kind of ecosystem such as those found in biology. Any biologist knows how unimaginably complex even the smallest ecosystem can be. Species multiply, compete over resources, feed off each other, develop niches, and then die off precipitously. The food chain of the smallest pond is immense. So, too, investors compete for access to markets and information, expend energy in attempts to reap extra resources, feed off each other's mistakes, develop specialties, and sometimes go bankrupt. This complexity of short-, medium-, and long-term trends all intersecting makes prediction very difficult. Not necessarily impossible, but very difficult.

J. Doyle Farmer, a pioneer in complex systems theory, studies this at the Santa Fe Institute. He also claims to beat the market on a regular basis with computer systems that buy and sell based on his proprietary techniques. He founded Prediction Company, which does technical trading for Warburg Dillon Read using advanced mathematical formulas and supercomputers. He appears to be exploiting inefficiencies, but not very large ones. Although he is not a devotee of the Efficient Market Theory, he concedes that markets are quite competitive. By his own admission, it would only take a handful of experts with a knack for mathematics and some very large computers before his profits would begin to decline significantly.

Farmer's program trading software looks for numerous little anomalies, and it takes many small positions. The fact that their trades are reliably profitable and so numerous, he points out, statistically proves that his technique is not luck. Still, this does little to aid the arguments of stock pickers. Farmer does not try to identify individual company success as do typical investment analysts. Complex systems theory suggests this is quite hard. His is not an approach for the masses, and it is not exploitable by many.

What defines a winner in such a fast-moving economy? Little things that snowball into an avalanche of success that no reasonable person could have predicted. That is why complex systems are so closely identified with chaos theory, or the theory that patterns tend to emerge out of apparent disorder. *The Tipping Point*, a recent bestseller by Malcolm Gladwell on little things that make a big difference or tip over the fence into a major event, has many such examples. A key business case it discusses is Airwalk, the sneaker company that snuck up on Nike and Adidas by cultivating a Southern California skateboard crowd and promoting its ethos nationally. "At its peak, Airwalk was ranked by one major marketing research company as the thirteenth 'coolest' brand among teenagers in the world, and the number three footwear brand, behind Nike and Adidas. Somehow, within the space of a year or two, Airwalk was jolted out of its quiet equilibrium on the beaches of southern California. In the mid-1990s, Airwalk tipped."[10]

So far, so good. Might there be a root cause for success? Well, first we had better examine the book's "short answer" for the source of success: advertising. The firm launched an "inspired advertising campaign" that showed the "Airwalk user relating to his shoes in some weird way." As a management strategy it might be called "management by weird promotion!" Contrarian marketing campaigns are wonderful tactics but not easily repeatable exercises, and they certainly do not constitute a management strategy. Imagine every brand manager at Proctor & Gamble trying to outdo each other in "weirdness" in product advertisements for their shampoos and deodorant. If everyone's product is made to seem weird, what's left for the rebels: promoting the normal?

As a chronicle of the extraordinary, *The Tipping Point* makes wonderful background reading for the person interested in complex systems. It has many of examples of social phenomena that spread like wildfire for reasons that were not obvious to observers at the time. (All phenomena seem obvious in hindsight.)

One problem with this entertaining book is one that pervades the media and the investor world: lack of knowledge of the basics of current theory. *The Tipping Point* is very much a book about complex systems, sociology, and perhaps chaos theory as applied in human endeavors. Somehow the author, a former *Washington Post* business and science writer currently working for the *New Yorker*, barely mentions them. Sociologists have been tossing around ideas like this for decades. The notion of *memes,* or the passing on of an idea or behavior pattern from person to person within a culture, is a quarter century old. Instead, pseudo science is created around extraordinary events: "*The Tipping Point* is the biography of an idea . . . that the best way to understand the emergence of fashion trends . . . or any number of other mysterious changes that mark everyday life is to think of them as epidemics. Ideas and products and messages and behaviors spread just like viruses."

Perhaps it is entertaining to envision change in the natural world through metaphors, but the virus metaphor strikes me as particularly uninformative. Few entities in nature change as quickly and strikingly as the virus. How do we describe the effect of an entity whose role in life is to adapt to its surroundings? By definition, any description will be obsolete before the pen hits the paper. The virus metaphor describes the exact opposite: that which cannot be identified by a set of patterns but is rather a reflection of the original object at hand. Notably and understandably absent in this book is any attempt to predict future outcomes based on its assertions. Such books do not help to spread deeper understanding of business and finance.

Even those who espouse other theories to explain market behavior, including those few economists who take issue with the logic of the Efficient Market Theory, almost universally agree that competition is stiff and a free lunch is hard to come by. Their conclusion once again is that typical investors are not likely to beat the market with a clever stock-picking fund manager, especially after fees are subtracted.

CHAPTER 7

Clash of the Titans

*In the real world, investors seem to have great difficulty
outperforming one another in any convincing or consistent
fashion. Today's hero is often tomorrow's blockhead.*

—Peter L. Bernstein, *Against the Gods*

There is perhaps no more telling comparison of indexing to active investing than by placing Fidelity Magellan side-by-side with the Vanguard S&P 500. As of 2002, these were the two largest funds in the United States, at $77 billion and $70 billion, respectively. The first is the champion of active funds over the last 25 years, whereas the second is the long-standing leader in large-cap indexing. The comparison is so instructive because on the face of it, Magellan is the clear winner in annualized returns versus Vanguard S&P from the day they both competed. If you went back and invested money at the very beginning of Magellan's life, here's what you would have ended up with compared to Vanguard (shown in Figure 7.1).

However, does that reflect what investors reasonably could have benefited from in practical terms? As we shall see, Magellan's paper advantage rests on a host of assumptions that should be examined. First, a little background is in order.

FIGURE 7.1   VANGUARD S&P VERSUS MAGELLAN—
                  TOTAL RETURNS

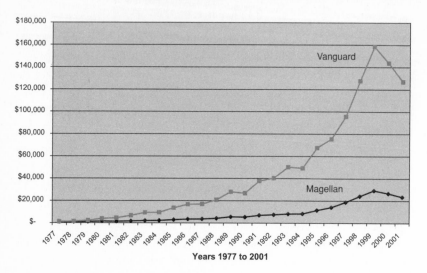

Years 1977 to 2001

Includes all annual expenses but not sales loads.
SOURCE: VFINX data courtesy of Morningstar; FMAGX data courtesy of Fidelity.

Magellan is an active fund with a storied history. Its manager from 1977 to 1990 was the legendary Peter Lynch, a freethinking and candid individual whose accounts of the fund's wild ride are revealing. During his tenure he accumulated what many consider to be the finest record as a manager in the history of U.S. mutual funds. In bull market and bear, he was able to find and ride on the coattails of industrial firms with steady earnings, as well as sidestep some of the worst corrections by under-weighting sectors about to be hit hardest.

The fund began auspiciously when in 1976 tiny Magellan, with only $6 million, was merged with Essex Fund, which had once been a proud $100 million fund but had suffered terrible losses and had more in tax losses to carry forward ($18 million) than assets under management. Magellan investors were the instant recipients of this tax shelter windfall. Over his career with Magellan, Lynch admits to no particular technique beyond individual stock picking: "The fact is that I never had an overall strategy. My stock picking was entirely empirical, and I went sniffing from one case to another like a bloodhound that's trained to follow a scent."[1] By his own admission much of his success is due not to what individual stocks he picked but what asset classes he avoided (remember the Brinson study highlighting the importance of asset allocation?). He was underweight in cyclical stocks when they were hit hard in the downturn of 1987: "I began to de-emphasize the autos and upgrade the financial companies—particularly Fannie Mae, but also the S&Ls." He pared back his S&L positions before the crash came.

He also doesn't pretend that he could see market corrections such as the one in 1987: "Here the market was wildly overvalued and poised for a 1000-point decline—a situation that is obvious in hindsight—yet with my usual clairvoyance about the Big Picture, I managed to miss it." Lastly, Lynch fully admits that his fund was more risky than the S&P 500: ". . . whenever the stock market did poorly, Magellan did worse." In other words, Magellan needed to outperform the S&P 500 to justify its risk.

Regarding the size of Magellan, Lynch says he was motivated to run such an increasingly unwieldy fund by wanting to prove his critics wrong. "They said a billion was too big, then 2 billion, 4, 6, 8 and 10 billion, and all along I was determined to prove them wrong," he writes. The fund owners, Fidelity Investments, may have been encouraged to accept new investment by something more than just the challenge. There were enormous management fees at stake: "Other hedge funds had closed the door to new share-holders once these funds had reached a certain size, but Magellan was kept open, and even this was perceived as a negative. The critics said it was Fidelity's way of capitalizing on my reputation and attracting more fees."[2]

Lynch has appeared prominently in advertisements for Fidelity for more than a decade following his retirement, during which time Fidelity took in enormous fees. At an average expense ratio of 0.88% and $50 billion in assets, its annual revenues stand at a cool $67 million, and that does not count a substantial 3% commission on all new cash (the fund is closed to new investors but accepts funds from old ones and is still growing). Lynch may have been driven by a desire to prove critics wrong by outperforming the market with a large fund, but the owners of Fidelity may have been driven more by the bottom line.

On the Vanguard side, the story has been equally remarkable. Vanguard Group is a curious entity. It's actually owned by the stockholders, so any excess profit for the year is returned to fund holders! Manager Gus Sauter's view on turnover and time horizon couldn't be more different than Lynch's: "The average holding period [among mutual funds] has gone from about 10 years to about 2½ years. It worries us. We do not think this is an appropriate way to try to save for goals. We think that longer time-horizon investing is the best way—certainly to achieve retirement goals. If you're forty years old, I'd say longer term would be 30 or 40 years horizon. Even if you're 60 years old, I'd say it's 20 years. It's certainly not 2½ years."[3]

Sauter does see problems with large active funds such as Magellan: "It used to be called the 'Peter Lynch effect.' He created such a big fund that by the time he was done buying a stock he himself had driven the price up. That kind of momentum can last for a period of time. But there are other periods of time when that type of investing does very poorly. Janus has been riding a very strong wave," said Sauter. This statement was made during the heyday of the technology bubble, and subsequently Janus did take a hard fall.

Jack Bogle, founder of Vanguard, confirms that the group's position is to constantly find efficiencies and pass them on to investors: The lower-priced funds have been raising their fees. We are seeing price competition, but the competition is to raise prices, not lower them. Mutual fund managers want to spend more on marketing and make more."[4]

Of course, at Vanguard S&P there is no stock picking (the group does operate a few inexpensive active funds) and no attempt to sidestep down markets. However, the management team is very good at keeping expenses low, not letting changes to the index squeeze it, and minimizing taxes. There seems to be no downside to size for them.

Gus Sauter, quoted from IndexFunds.com, notes, "We're unique in the mutual fund industry in that the people who invest in our funds actually own us. So what we would make as profit we turn back over to them in the form of lower expense ratios. We merely operate at cost. Whatever it costs us to operate the funds, including our salaries and everything else, we only charge that amount to the funds themselves—so Vanguard essentially breaks even every year."

FIGURE 7.2   VANGUARD VERSUS MAGELLAN AFTER TAX AND
SALES LOAD

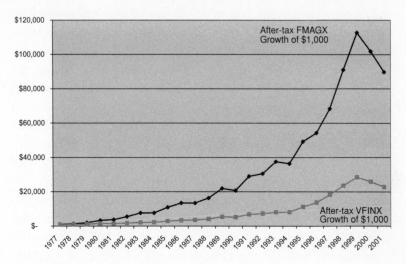

Now let's return to the numbers. Since Vanguard came along later, we start the comparison at its inception in 1976. We graciously ignore the fact that another unsuccessful fund was merged with Magellan.

The first chart we examined, 7.1, shows returns are net of annual expenses, including management fees. Currently annual expense ratios stand at 0.18% for Vanguard and 0.88% for Magellan. Now we need to account for Magellan's front sales load. It has shrunk over time to 3%, but in 1976 it was an astounding 8.5%! The results dampen Magellan's performance, as shown in Figure 7.2.

Now need to adjust for taxes. As with all tax analysis, differences in individual investor federal and state tax rates can be substantial: we picked intermediate assumptions. We were unable to get precise figures from Fidelity, so we apply a conservative 100% turnover, based on Lynch's description of his trading practices, declining over time to the current 24%. We give Vanguard a constant 5% turnover. There is no question that Fidelity had rather high turnover early on and quite a bit less later on, but always more than Vanguard. We account for changing tax rates, especially in regard to capital gains. Now the story is again different (see Figure 7.2). Vanguard creeps closer.

These are the comparative returns, on paper. Now we should note that to get these returns Magellan took on greater risk, and indeed, so would the investor at the time of investment. On one side we have a fund that replicates the largest companies in the stock market, and on the other side we have a fund that received a boost in assets from other failed funds and is soon to receive a new manager. Which fund would have been the riskier choice from the investor's point of view? We think the answer is obvious.

Thus far we have assumed that all investment goes into each fund in 1977. But that is not what happened. Most money came in far later. So we may count the actual dollars made, not the percentage improvement. As we might have expected, Magellan's most spectacular percentage gains were earlier in its life, and the bulk of its money came later.

As Figures 7.3 and 7.4 show, Vanguard S&P 500 performed quite well during the critical late 1990s when the funds were largest. Both funds were relatively small until the late 1980s.

FIGURE 7.3   PERCENTAGE RETURNS FOR MAGELLAN AND VANGUARD S&P

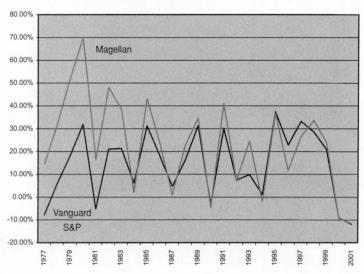

This brings up the critical issue of how an investor could have spotted Magellan as the future star that it became. Let's assume that Lynch was a brilliant stock picker. Only a clairvoyant would have been able to see that, absent performance to the contrary. By his own admission, he had no set strategy, so he couldn't have convinced investors he had a better plan to beat the market. In addition, waiting 5 or 10 years to be sure of his performance would have lost most of the great years of Magellan. The fact is that there were many funds with good records at the time. Also, most investors add to their funds. It turns out that the two funds become comparable for investors who add to their funds gradually, or dollar cost average. This is demonstrated in Figure 7.5, where investors starting in 1981 or 1987 added $1,000 adjusted for inflation each year.

Now let us fast-forward to today. Magellan still has a superior record to the S&P 500 over the long run, and if this is to be our guide, why shouldn't the investor just plunge in? Because it is easy to show that the Magellan of today isn't even trying to outperform Vanguard. It's a closet index fund that tracks the S&P 500 remarkably closely. Let us start with a simple examination of the two funds' composition as of early 2002, as shown in Table 7.1.

FIGURE 7.4   FUND ASSETS ($ BILLIONS) COMPARISON

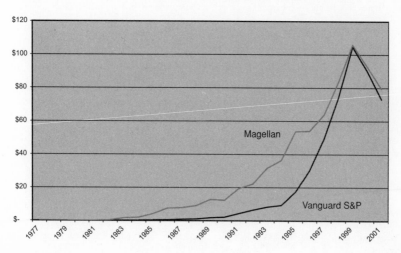

FIGURE 7.5   DOLLAR COST AVERAGE INVESTING
COMPARISONS 5 AND 10 YEARS AFTER LYNCH
STARTS AT MAGELLAN

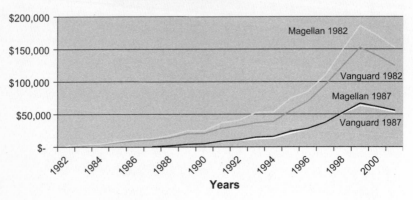

TABLE 7.1   IDENTICAL HOLDINGS BETWEEN MAGELLAN AND
S&P 500 AMONG MAGELLAN TOP 10 STOCKS

NAME OF HOLDING	% OF FUND/INDEX HELD BY BOTH MAGELLAN AND S&P 500
General Electric	3.78%
Citigroup	2.47%
American Intl Grp	1.97%
ExxonMobil	2.55%
Tyco Intl	1.12%
Pfizer	2.38%
Microsoft	3.39%
Wal-Mart Stores	2.00%
Total	**19.66%**

SOURCE: Vanguard 500 data as of 12/31/01, Magellan data as of 9/30/01.
The 3 month difference is due to the fact that Vanguard reports the holdings of its funds more
frequently than Fidelity. Mutual funds are only required to disclose holdings twice a year.

And that's only commonality among Magellan's top ten. The fact is that a significant portion of both funds is absolutely identical, share for share. For this portion, performance has to be the same. Now let's place the funds next to each other in a graph, in Figure 7.6.

Clearly, their movements are not far apart.

A mathematically precise way to see how alike the funds are is to calculate the correlation of their price movements over time. This is done by placing many months of daily closing prices next to each other and calculating what is called an R-Squared statistic. It is a form of correlation that reveals the degree to which one series of data can be "explained" by another. A result of 100% means the two pairs of data move in lockstep. In recent years the number has hovered around 95%, and it was 94% when we last checked. In other words, one fund moves 94% in harmony with the other. They are likely to produce identical returns at the end of the period, before fees and taxes. Any deviation is likely to be random and small. Since Vanguard has such a fee and tax advantage, it is almost guaranteed to win. The point is that day-by-day and month-by-month the funds move together. There is just as much probability that one will out-

FIGURE 7.6   MAGELLAN VERSUS VANGUARD RETURNS

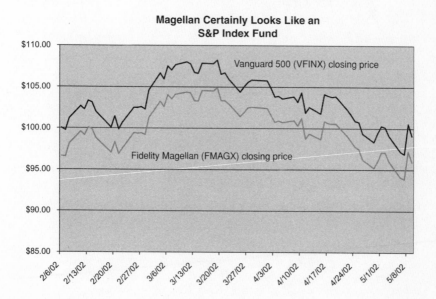

perform the other before fees according to most economists. This deviation will almost certainly be less than 6% and in fact is likely to be no more than a few percentage points per year. So why would anyone pay a 3% sales fee and 0.7% more per year in expenses in this hopeless quest? Ignorance and the power of Wall Street marketing are the only answers we can come up with.

Today the race to the top of the asset hill is still running strong. In early 2001, just as the world was celebrating the new millennium, the Vanguard S&P 500 was poised to become the largest fund in the world, eclipsing the legendary Fidelity Magellan Fund. Indexers, including those on our site, were gleeful about the upstart indexer trouncing the pillar of stock-picking prowess. Vanguard's fund was the brainchild of indexing pioneer John Bogle and to many of us the beacon of strength for all indexers. Finally, on April 5, 2001, Vanguard S&P 500 became the largest fund in the world with $107.2 billion in assets, surpassing Magellan at $106.9 billion, according to *fidelityinvestor.com*.

It didn't stay on the podium long. During the market drops of 2000 and 2001, Vanguard S&P 500 shed assets sharply. In retrospect, it shouldn't have been our beacon, because all indexers should have known that there is more to the discipline than the S&P 500. This silly little race was an apt reminder. As if it really mattered, Vanguard's victory is ultimately assured. Time is on its side. The Magellan Fund is closed to new investors, because unlike Vanguard, Magellan is making concentrated bets on a few stocks at a time. It is having a hard enough time investing its money as it is. Popularity for the S&P 500 will come back soon enough.

Results of this comparison may come as a surprise to many readers. That's because most investors have access to Fidelity's sanitized, polished account of Magellan's success. Yes, in some abstract, theoretical sense, Magellan was superior. It made more money for a very small cadre of extremely lucky investors. For the bulk, however, it did no better and often worse. And today there is little reason to pay Magellan's high fee so long as it continues to be a closet S&P 500 index fund.

CHAPTER 8

A Mountain of Evidence

"Active Management is a beauty contest in which the aver-age contestant is kind of ugly."

—John Rekenthaler, *Morningstar*

There is voluminous evidence to examine when considering whether individual investors can beat the market indexes with publicly available mutual funds after paying 1% or 2% in extra fees. Likewise, when traders are compared against nontraders, the latter always come out ahead. Trading fees seem to be the obvious culprit. There are literally hundreds of studies that tackle the question from a variety of approaches.

To examine this subject fully would require a separate, much larger volume than this one. The beginning indexer easily could get lost trying to gain comprehensive knowledge of this extensive subject. There is always time later to return to it to plow through all the nitty-gritty details. For this journey, probably no better single catalog of studies exists than the classic *A Random Walk Down Wall Street* by Professor Burton Malkiel at Princeton University. In this chapter we highlight one or two leading studies in each category of inquiry.

Keep in mind that no reputable study has *ever* shown that on average investors can consistently beat their target benchmarks after paying the hefty annual fees of today's typical active fund.

We make it one of our top priorities at IndexFunds.com to chase down studies that compare active versus index investing. If you hear of a legitimate study that claims to show active investing beating its passive alternative, we really want to know! It would truly be sensational news, and we want to be the first to print it. We might even get a Nobel prize in economics if we could produce a theory to unseat efficient markets. Every time we rush out to verify a claim of a strategy that shows how star fund managers outsmart the market, we invariably come away disappointed. Whenever we study star managers, the case for passive indexing comes out looking stronger.

Curiously, Wall Street conducts very little research into this subject. It's as if Ford Motors decided it wasn't worth it to crash-test its cars to see if they were safe, or as if Proctor & Gamble felt it didn't need to conduct focus groups to see if people really were satisfied with its shampoos. Yes, the work can be painstaking and requires attention to detail, and advanced statistics. But this is not the reason Wall Street is uninterested or unable to pursue the work. Wall Street's concern, obviously, is that they might not find the answers they are looking for.

The occasional study by a Wall Street firm tends to pick a very limited question, stir up the pot of data a bit, and serve up a lukewarm brew of inconclusive results that reaffirm the status quo of expensive actively managed funds. Often, the evidence is so strong they are forced to acknowledge the power of indexing.

The "Core and Explore" study of 1999 by Charles Schwab, the discount brokerage firm, is a case in point. Despite being awash in sales commissions of actively managed funds, it is a relatively progressive brokerage firm. It found itself obligated to recommend that investors make their "core" holdings index funds, and only then to "explore" with active funds in an attempt to beat markets.[1]

The Schwab study also concluded that active managers have an advantage over indexing in international markets. This referred to nothing more than the practice of sidestepping the hugely overvalued Japan market to best the MSCI (Morgan Stanley Capital International), EAFE (Europe, Australasia, Far East) index. Any indexer could have done the same by selecting indexes that exclude Japan. Anyway, despite being a rather lightweight study, it does generally support indexing.

Anyone with access to Wiesenberger or Morningstar data (these firms track funds for a fee) can perform a basic comparison of active to index funds. For one-year performance, over the past several decades the S&P has reliably beaten managers about two-thirds of the time. The last 10 years display the following pattern, as shown in Table 8.1. Because of this consistent average superiority, longer periods tend to emphasize the index fund advantage. For instance, dividing 40 years from 1962 to 2001 into five-year runs, the S&P 500 has beaten the average large-cap fund in five of eight periods, including all of the last four stretches since 1981. The longer the period you examine, the more likely it becomes that indexes will come out on top.

TABLE 8.1   CALENDAR YEAR PERFORMANCE OF ALL
             LARGE BLEND DOMESTIC STOCK FUNDS AGAINST
             S&P 500, 1992–2001

YEAR	TOTAL AVERAGE RETURN OF ALL LARGE-CAP BLEND FUNDS	(+) OR (–) TO S&P 500 RETURN
1992	8.13%	0.51%
1993	11.10%	1.04%
1994	−0.63%	−1.95%
1995	32.36%	−5.17%
1996	21.06%	−1.89%
1997	27.73%	−5.625
1998	22.54%	−6.04%
1999	20.70%	−0.34%
2000	−6.48%	2.62%
2001	−13.52%	−1.64%

SOURCE: Morningstar data as of 4/30/2002

Almost all of the serious studies are performed by independent researchers, typically by academics, or financial consulting firms, or researchers at reputable independent firms. They may spend years organizing data, matching up funds with appropriate benchmarks, and looking for flaws in their assumptions. Most such studies are open to peer review, and many are rerun independently to verify results. I think they also thoroughly enjoy tweaking the nose of Wall Street professionals. Unfortunately, most of the studies are rather dry, and many contain reams of Greek symbols and advanced economic jargon.

For truly serious and valid studies, there are several requirements. To begin with, the study must account for survivorship. You may recall the pervasive practice by mutual funds of "seeding and weeding" discussed previously. Funds methodically seed new funds and then weed out the losers by merging their assets into the winners. In so doing, fund groups can be assured a constant new crop of stars. Valid studies must tally up the records not only of successful, existing actively managed funds but also of those funds that did poorly and are now defunct. This requires a little historical digging.

Fund groups prefer to quickly kill off funds that do poorly, normally accomplished by merging the fund's assets with a successful one of the same group. This is perfectly understandable because it is harder for a broker to sell poor performance than good. Funds do have minimum costs of operation. What is not understandable is failing to account for failed funds, which many Wall Street-sponsored studies prefer to do. The advertisement by a mutual fund group that they have highly rated funds generally covers over the fact that they have merged assets from previous losers into their stars.

When the inevitable failures are counted, active funds as a whole fare far worse. A comprehensive study of the 1962 to 1993 period by Mark Carhart, published in the prestigious *Journal of Finance*, found that by 1993 fully one-third of all funds launched during that time period had disappeared.[2] As investors chase star fund managers with increasing fervor, I expect this trend to increase. There simply is no room for also-rans. Accounting for these weeded-out funds inevitably will drag down the average performance of actively managed funds as a whole. Don't take any study on its face value that ignores survivorship.

In addition, any meaningful study on the fund performance must account for the different amounts of money in various funds. It's not the average performance of the fund that counts, it's the average performance of the dollar invested. For example, if a tiny fund beats the benchmark they are targeting and one giant fund does poorer, does that mean active funds in this sample have beaten the market? If one is looking at the average performance, it does! Thus, it is essential to weight performance by the assets in the fund.

It turns out that if you look at nearly any supersuccessful fund, it performs well while relatively small, and its performance wanes as its assets grow. Inevitably, the dollar-weighted performance of star funds are not what they appear to be on paper. How many investors jumped in at the beginning just before the fund took off? Very few. How many piled on late in the game just before the fund slacked off? The majority. Thus, the average return per dollar typically is far less than the average percentage return.

Another aspect of any thoughtful study is a fair-minded handling of historical data. There is no hard-and-fast rule here. With so many ups and downs in the market, it is very easy to select periods of strength (and ignore periods of weakness) that tend to jack up returns and/or downplay risks. This is called *data mining*. With the advent of the personal computer and extensive fund returns data, it is possible to sift through millions of combinations of different periods in time looking for the perfect result. Data mining, this strategy is often used to "prove" that a certain investing strategy is superior to indexing. The problem is that the one particular period selected for the study is the *only* period for which the thesis holds. This is why reputable comparative studies usually look at many different periods and base conclusions on an average.

Let us drill down to greater detail regarding studies of comparative performance to see the surprising extent of the damage. Because there is so much data on manager performance versus the market, it turns out that it is possible to crunch very revealing numbers. Broadly speaking, money managers do not keep up with broad benchmarks. One of the more recent studies going way back in time is by Ira Weiss, assistant accounting professor at Columbia Business School. He examined 36 years of mutual fund performance through 1997 and weighted his findings both for defunct funds and for actual dollars invested. Since some of the stock funds were able to hold higher-performing small stocks not found in the S&P, they had a built-in advantage. Diversified U.S. stock funds obtained a 10.2% average annualized return, far behind the 11.6% return for the S&P 500. It just so happens that the average fund fee was 1.4% in 2001, so in this case the managers appeared to trail the market by about the same percentage as their fees. Most studies suggest that managers trail their respective benchmarks by more than the cost of their fees. They actually do harm to their clients and get paid for it.

There are many other studies like this, all pointing to similar conclusions regarding average long-term performance. Burton Malkiel catalogs many of them in *Random Walk*.

Some brash managers insist they are different from the rest of the pack and point to their superior performance as proof. Keep in mind that by virtue of the laws of statistics, a certain number of managers must outperform the market in any period. The question is: Does the star manager tend to repeat superior performance or perform randomly in the future? A whole group of studies has tried to find predictable patterns among money managers. This is of key importance to individual investors because so many go about investing by selecting star mutual fund managers in expectations of beating the market above and beyond the hefty fees they frequently earn.

Mark Carhart's 1997 study of mutual funds from 1962 to 1993, published in the *Journal of Finance*, showed that momentum carried top funds for about a year or so before evaporating. The performance of these funds after that was entirely random. Carhart's conclusion was that there is no indication of skill among the winning fund managers, just the ability to ride the wave for a while. If you can ride new waves on a frequent basis, you might consistently beat the averages. Otherwise, forget about it. The Sharpe study on the performance of managers highly rated by Morningstar, discussed in the previous Chapter 5, came to essentially the same conclusion.

A whole slew of studies have confirmed the conclusion in regard to professional analysts as well as funds. This failure is essentially an indictment of the ability to easily gain outsized returns, from the most respected form of financial analysis, fundamental analysis of individual stocks. Buy and sell recommendations of analysts are poor predictors of the future. These recommendations are public and disseminated immediately so they can be tracked by a diligent researcher. According to Malkiel: "Bluntly stated, the careful estimates of security analysts (based on industry studies, plant visits, etc.) do little better than those that would be obtained by simple extrapolation of past trends, which we have already seen are no help at all. Indeed, when compared with actual earnings growth rates, the five-year estimates of security analysts were actually worse than the predictions from several naïve forecasting models."[3]

Malkiel's work in this area mimicked a drug test. The analysts' forecasts were the "drug," and the assumption that earnings growth rates would follow the long-run rate of growth in the U.S. economy (naïve forecasting model) was the "placebo." The placebo did as well as the drug. He found very poor short-term forecasting, and little consistency among them. That is, there did not even appear to be truly talented individuals among this already elite crowd. Harvard, MIT, or Stanford; it doesn't seem to matter. Researchers at these and other fine schools have all come up with similar results. Highly trained, experienced finance professionals with unrivaled access to company information do no better than what a first-year economics student might fashion out of a textbook.

It is possible that some investors are getting access to analyst recommendations quicker than others. A mutual fund that places many orders through a brokerage firm is likely to get a front-row seat before the analysts' speeches on a new company report and will be included in private conference calls that ordinary citizens might not be privy to. Is it possible that they will get winks and nods from analysts about which stocks they should buy before official recommendations are put out to the larger public? Possibly, but don't think that the analysts' firms won't try to charge for this privilege in some fashion.

Probably *the* most popular and respected method of picking stocks, fundamental analysis, rose to prominence in the 1940s and 1950s under respected analysts Benjamin Graham and David Dodd. It focuses on a company's income statement, balance sheet, and expected future financial performance. This discipline then projects forward earnings and cash flows and the risk of failing to identify firms whose current stock price seems inexpensive. Therefore, firms that are expected to grow their earnings and cash flows are more valuable than ones whose earnings and cash flows are expected to remain flat.

Fundamental analysis is highly respected as a method for stock analysis, and therefore attracts more of the finest minds in Wall Street. As a result, it is very hard to come up with truly important new information about a firm since so many other individuals are seeking the same thing. Inevitably, a general consensus begins to develop about a firm, its prospects, and the fairness of its valuation relative to other firms. That is why Wall Street professionals so often to refer to "analysts' consensus" on earnings projections. These projections rarely vary by much from one analyst to another.

Perhaps for this reason, fundamental analysis appears to have very little tangible value to the actual investor in Burton Malkiel's research. Deep thought about an individual firm is unlikely to produce information of sufficient value to justify the cost of that thought. The analysts themselves may have unique access to company management, but these rules are changing, as the SEC is beginning to insist that company conference calls be truly public. In addition, unique access and insight do not always translate into superior projections.

Another area of active strategies is charting, or technical analysis. This is the art of watching stock price trends, individually or as a group, for patterns or signals, which are then used to predict future market direction. Note that pure technicians do not care at all for the underlying valuation of the company or companies. They assume that all this information has been incorporated into prices, whose trends will reveal the likely course of the future. If they are right more than half of the time, it should be possible to outperform the market.

This practice is particularly derided by researchers for its flimsy theoretical basis. Its practical results are equally poor, according to Malkiel. Numerous elaborate schemes for analyzing charts have been devised, and none of them have stood up to scrutiny. Researchers will typically take an investment strategy and exhaustively apply it across massive numbers of stocks through numerous different time periods to back-test it. In this way enough data is generated to give statistical confidence about whether the strategy holds merit. Of course, the strategy must not just be profitable, it must beat the appropriate benchmark, and it must account for transaction costs.

The simplest pattern to look for is momentum. In physics, the law of momentum dictates that mass moving through space will continue to do so until friction slows it down. In the stock market the expression describes how a stock market going up is more likely to keep going up than down, and vice versa for a bear market that is going down. Unfortunately, there is no easily exploitable momentum. If a certain degree of correlation exists between past stock movements and subsequent ones, it is too short, irregular and small to be of any use to a trader who has to incur transaction costs.

A more elaborate strategy also filters out small, presumably less clear indications of momentum in favor of larger ones. For instance, a filter might only buy stocks that have shown 5% recent appreciation or sell stocks that have fallen 5%. This strategy is just as likely to buy high and sell low than correctly time market movement.

There are many more strategies based on signals with bizarre names such as breakouts, arms, shoulders, plateaus, peaks, valleys, ranges, moving averages, double tops, and triple tops. Technicians throw these and many more into a verbal cauldron of financial alchemy. It is possible to assess individual techniques but virtually impossible to judge the claims by technicians, since they themselves depend on "judgment" and constantly hop in and out of strategies based on inspiration and instinct. There is an almost tribal and animistic aspect to the technical community that is fascinating and, of course, completely ridiculous.

Information need not come strictly from prices. Analyzing trading volume is a favorite piece of market information considered by technicians. Heavy trading regardless of price movements is thought to reveal that smart money (some of which could involve insider information) has learned important new information. But it is equally true that seasonal and random jumps in volume occur for all stocks, and trading in smaller companies can be especially lumpy as relatively large blocks by founders are unloaded. Studies show that investors will have an impossible task trying to separate the wheat from the chaff: What is high volume based on random investor allocation decisions and what is volume driven by profound knowledge about the company's prospects?

Insider trading is another bit of nonprice information that sparks everyone's interest. Everyone can agree that it exists, that is, anyone who has followed the Enron debacle, in which executives sold their shares in a hurry even as they were papering over losses incurred with secretive energy deals. So if it can be tracked accurately it should be possible to create a profitable trading strategy. This appeals to any investor frustrated with the fog of the market where nothing seems certain. If anyone knows what is going on, it must be the executives. Adding to the allure of this trading strategy is the fact that extensive data based on publicly disclosed sales by insiders is available. Unfortunately, insiders sell for all sorts of reasons that have more to do with their personal life than the company: They want to build a vacation house, they need to prepare for estate taxes, or they are going through a messy divorce. And they may buy unwisely because of pride. Once again, it is hard to separate the good information from the bad. And if someone truly is selling due to inside knowledge, they have taken the first bit of potential profit out of the market. Finally, analyzing insider sales is time-consuming and expensive, further lowering potential net profits. As a result, there is no study to indicate that the average investor can profit from funds that follow insider trading.

There is an unlimited number of strategies to try to outsmart the market. Funds that defy easy description but are free to invest in virtually any speculative strategy they see fit are lumped into the category of hedge funds. They can profit handsomely by correctly calling a bear market, but over the long haul studies have shown they tend to bring mediocre returns. At the same time, they are extremely expensive and quite risky. "In one respect, hedge fund managers are no different from any other asset manager. When things go well, it is ascribed to their own brilliance; when things go wrong, it is the market's fault for moving against them."[4]

The most celebrated hedge fund manager in recent history, George Soros, gained fame for his daring showdown against the British Treasury in 1992 when he speculated against the pound and forced it into a humiliating devaluation. Unfortunately, his recent track record has been far less stellar. His flagship Quantum Fund, which held assets of over $6 billion in 1999, suffered three successive years of decline at a time when

U.S. equities were shooting through the roof. His smaller Quota Fund suffered a 46% drop in 1998. Despite highly publicized successes earlier in the decade with smaller funds, later in the 1990s his larger funds took severe hits. Because of this, it is open to debate just how strong his returns have been over time for the average dollar invested under his care. I would hazard a guess that they are not nearly as strong as his reputation.

So much for hiring money managers, but what about picking your own stocks? There is nothing wrong with buying your own stocks, so long as you diversify, avoid stockpicking and buy for the long term. In other words, create your own index. Terrance Odean, assistant professor at the University of California, Berkeley, and Brad Barber, assistant professor at the University of California, Davis, examined 60,000 actual returns of households which traded stocks with a discount broker. "The average household tilts their common stock investment toward high-beta, small, value stocks, and turns over 80 per cent of their portfolio annually," they noted.[5]

The average household earned 15.3%, whereas a benchmark weighted towards value in the same manner as the households delivered 17.7%. When they divided households into groups based on their trading behavior, the traders trailed badly. The most frenetic 20% of households earned only a 10.0% return. They concluded that: "The poor performance of those households that trade frequently is generally consistent with the implications of recent theoretical models of investor overconfidence. Our central message is that trading is hazardous to your wealth."

Highly confident men dominate both day-trading and Wall Street, which may explain why men so clearly underperform women as investors. Yes, that's right. Male overconfidence is at the root of underperformance with individual investors, according to Odean and Barber's delightful follow-up February 2001 study on male versus female performance, "Boys Will Be Boys: Gender, Overconfidence, and Common Stock Investment," also in the *Quarterly Journal of Economics*.[6] Its findings were summarized crisply: "Psychological research has established that men are more prone to overconfidence than women. Thus, models of investor overconfidence predict that men will trade more and perform worse than women. Using account data for over 35,000 households from a large discount brokerage firm, we analyze the common stock investments of men and women from February 1991 through January 1997. Consistent with the predictions of the overconfidence models, we document that men trade 45 percent more than women and earn annual risk-adjusted net returns that are 1.4 percent less than those earned by women. These differences are more pronounced between single men and single women; single men trade 67 percent more than single women and earn annual risk-adjusted net returns that are 2.3 percent less than those earned by single women."

The best evidence is about publicly available mutual funds or individuals. Less clear is the record concerning institutional pension fund investing and especially private family funds. "At the institutional level, it has been difficult to obtain data enabling a fair comparison between index and active funds after management charges," wrote PriceWaterhouseCoopers, the accounting firm, in a 1997 study on the subject. "For this reason, it is doubtful that pension fund sponsors fully appreciate the extent to which index funds are efficient in terms of the risk/return tradeoff."

For pension funds studies generally show indexing as superior at the various risk levels involved. For private equity funds, such as portfolios of wealthy clients, private universities, or other entities, it is an open question but plausible that they underperform standard index funds on a risk-adjusted basis. But if they do, it is no doubt because they suffer few of the same constraints.

They have few marketing, legal compliance, or customer service costs. They have no constraints on asset classes. If a private equity money manager sees good buys in commercial real estate, it's no problem. They may buy the building directly. If exotic fixed-income instruments such as leasing of manufacturing plant and equipment seem appealing, they often have a free hand there, too. Many private equity clients have very long time horizons, hire specialized professionals to monitor their holdings, and are often sophisticated investors in their own right. They are comfortable with any asset class as long as it pays sufficiently well and has the risk profile being sought. Flexibility in choosing assets can really make a dent in taxation as well. Commercial real estate especially can be a great tax shield, but its complexity has kept it from becoming a major part of the mutual fund industry.

Private investment management requires a large portfolio to be able to afford certain economies of scale. What does a private equity fund pay for continual analysis of its portfolio by the very best private money managers and consultants that can be found? Only about 0.10% of one percent of assets per year was the answer of one representative of a multibillion dollar private equity fund. There is no way that average individual investors could buy that kind of asset allocation advice. Their portfolio would be eaten up in a few years by fees. However, even though private equity portfolios may not consist of traditional indexes, a closer look reveals they are quite passive in nature. Office buildings, small companies, and blocks of fixed-income instruments are bought and held for many years to keep middlemen costs down and obtain favorable tax treatment. Many such active investment groups share much with indexing.

In summary, the evidence of indexing's superiority for the typical investor is overwhelming. It is for the active crowd to lay out a convincing case that they can beat index funds. They are, after all, asking the investor to take the extra risk. Even before fees, the record simply doesn't give them much room. After fees, it is a hopeless argument.

CHAPTER 9

Tenancious Myths Debunked

"Lake Wobegon, where all the women are strong, all the men are good looking, and all the children are above average."

—Garrison Keilor, National Public Radio

Perhaps it is the nature of indexing or perhaps it is the powerful marketing by Wall Street, but there are some myths about the supposed virtue of active investing and weakness of indexing that just won't seem to go away! I list them here for easy reference even though many are touched on elsewhere in the book. You are invited to scan the list. If they all seem obviously false, this chapter may be skipped. If any seem plausible or even mildly convincing, read more closely to carefully consider assumptions you are making and your financial thought process! Every myth that follows has been debunked conclusively and can be dangerous to an investor's program.

MYTH #1: INDEXING WORKS IN UP BUT NOT IN DOWN MARKETS

When stocks are climbing, goes the story, it is easy enough to ride the tide with all boats. However, in a bear market there are fewer winners, and the professionals are the best ones to find them. It seems to make sense, which may explain the popularity of this myth. The problem with avoiding bad stocks in down markets is the same problem with attempts to find good stocks in up markets. Everyone else is doing the same, and prices typically already reflect that. Market competition doesn't end just because the market has turned bearish.

If you truly don't want to invest in an asset class because it is showing very high valuations across the board, then you don't want a money manager anyway. Just pull your money out and put it in short-term bonds. However, consider first that market ups and downs are normally interspersed with swift movements occurring in a concentrated number of days. Markets don't offer continuous, easily blocked-out trends. Large swings may occur quickly and be over in a heartbeat, so trying to dodge bear markets is essentially a short-term trading strategy and the evidence shows it does not work reliably except in the most obviously overvalued markets, which occurs infrequently. Since in approximately four out of five days the market goes up, however haltingly, the task of picking that one day of retreat is pretty tough.

The data does not support the notion that one can trade one's way out of trouble in a down market. It was tested most recently in a clever way by Morningstar fund analyst Peter Di Teresa, who grouped 4880 domestic equity funds by turnover ratio and examined their performance over a one-year span ending on February 28, 2002. That coincides with a nasty bear market. Di Teresa compared the performance of funds in the top third in terms of turnover ratio against the bottom third. The highest-turnover group lost 10.5% over the year previous to February 28, 2002, whereas the lowest-turnover dropped only 6.3%.

This time, he took the same group of domestic stock funds and broke them up evenly by turnover into five groups. Turnover was correlated not with safety but rather with failure. The highest-turnover fund group (976 funds) finished down 11.5% for the year period, followed by the middle-turnover group, while the lowest-turnover group did best by losing only 5.8%. This is a pervasive myth, but without substance.

MYTH #2: INDEXING DOESN'T WORK IN A "STOCK PICKER'S MARKET"

In the United States this myth pops up every time small- and mid-cap indexes do better than the S&P 500. No sooner are results announced during such years than pundits proclaim that fund managers "beat the market." Of course, what happened was that funds on average tend to invest in smaller companies than the weighted average of the S&P, so they should be expected to do better on average. When compared against indexes of small- or mid-cap holdings, they reliably underperform the averages as a group.

MYTH #3: INDEXING WORKS BEST IN LARGE CAPS

At least this myth is based on plausible logic. The notion here is that information about large caps is more abundant and widely disseminated than information about small caps. Large-cap stocks generally have dozens of top-notch analysts modeling performance and posting recommendations for all to see, and far more fund managers sift through this information carefully. Small-cap stocks, on the other hand, may be lucky to have one or two analysts, and reports are likely to be far less thorough and widely read. Nearly every theory of market activity predicts there is more value to a fund manager reading reports and doing original research concerning companies that are less visible.

Unfortunately, the numbers don't show any better performance for active small-cap managers relative to their indexes than large-cap managers, especially after taxes.[1] One likely reason for this is that hidden transaction costs such as bid-ask spread and impact are greater in the small-cap arena, so any passive approach that limits turnover has a head start.

Impact costs in particular are a function of the size of the player's trades. With large stocks, buy or sell orders of tens of thousands of shares are no big deal, but with a small stock it's easy to see the elephants once they are in the vegetable garden. Nimble traders jump in front with small trades (which they turn around and dump on the pachyderms at a profit), and the available supply of willing sellers is exhausted quickly. The larger the fund, the more this phenomenon will occur.

MYTH #4: INTERNATIONAL ACTIVE MANAGERS CAN EASILY BEAT THE MARKET

This statement is usually made in reference to the ease with which international fund managers have soundly beaten the dominant international index, Morgan Stanley's EAFE (Europe, Australasia, and Far East), during the past 15 years. It is true in a shallow sense, but also meaningless. The way managers did it was not by stock picking. It was by one important asset allocation decision: avoid Japan after 1990.

In the 1970s and 1980s Japan was awash in cheap money (and still is, unfortunately) and encouraged cross-ownership of stock between companies that contributed to enormous real estate and equities inflation. Seemingly everyone could see it except the Japanese, who celebrated a huge runup prior to 1990 and then suffered a dismal and continuous dropoff for 12 years after 1990.

International fund managers have consistently underinvested in Japan. Prior to 1990 they bemoaned losing out on the phenomenal growth of that market. By 1990, EAFE was heavily weighted with Japanese firms and became a tough index to beat (because they were so massively inflated). Then, international fund managers began to love the fact that it was their benchmark. All they had to do was avoid obviously overvalued Japan to beat EAFE. It was like shooting fish in a barrel. This story shows the importance of the benchmark when comparing performance. The fund managers trounced an inappropriate index.

International stock indexes that did not contain Japan would have been a far better benchmark for these managers, and guess what? These indexes trounced the managers. For the managers who avoided the Japanese bubble, stock picking was not the reason for their success—asset allocation and avoidance of the bubble was.

At this point in the debate active managers charged foul play, claiming that they beat international indexing fair and square, and that was that. But international indexing does not equal EAFE any more than domestic indexing equals the S&P 500. A mature, thoughtful approach to indexing actually encourages examination of each and every asset class.

If an asset class is not attractive, then one can avoid it and choose an index that does not contain it. One can agree with analysts or money managers on the selection of asset classes but avoid their wasteful stock picking. Many indexers did just that by reading available research and watching active managers' movements. They then built portfolios of international index funds with Japan carved out and kept the high fees to themselves.

MYTH #5: INDEXING PUSHES UP THE MARKET

The charge here is that the popularity of indexing the S&P 500 led to extreme valuations, especially relative to small-cap stocks. The theory is that indexing the S&P 500 is a self-fulfilling prophecy. Companies that are added to the S&P 500 experience price spikes as passive investors necessarily snap up shares. In other words, added companies get pricier simply because they are index members, not because of fundamental economic reasons. As financial advisor Larry Swedroe pointed out on IndexFunds.com, the idea doesn't hold water. One study in the area was conducted in 1998 by Melissa Brown, former head of quantitative research at Prudential Securities. Contrary to popular belief, the proportion of S&P 500 Index fund assets declined from 6.7% in 1992 to 6.1% in 1997. The funds grew from $255 billion to $600 billion, but the rest of the market also grew. Similarly, Brown noted that there was a net outflow of investor capital. If all investors had kept their money in the funds the total return (price appreciation plus dividends) would have grown to $650 billion, or $50 billion more than it did.[1]

Swedroe ticks off no less than six studies from reputable researchers that examine various questions relating to indexing's effect on the market. Every single study finds little or no impact.[2]

MYTH #6: INDEXING IS ONLY FOR EQUITIES

As it turns out, indexing is even more relevant to bonds, real estate investment trusts, and other securities. There are a number of bond funds with modest fees that track well-known U.S. and international indexes. Common sense should tell any investor that keeping fees down is especially important in today's low-interest-rate environment where investors are loading up on bonds. A 1% fee on a bond fund that returns only 5% is a much bigger proportion of return than a 1% fee on an equity fund earning 14%.

Bond funds simply don't vary that much in return within their classes. Funds specializing in high-grade corporate bonds pretty much stick together, as do government-debt bonds and high-yield bonds (junk bonds). Credit rating agencies such as Mergent (formerly Moody's) and Standard & Poor's do a fairly good job on average of rating companies' risk of default. They fail to catch firms such as Enron who are less creditworthy than they seem, but by and large they prove a better bellwether of success than equity analysts' earnings estimates.

This is no surprise since the credit rating agencies have fewer obvious conflicts of interest, as they do not offer investment banking services to the same firms they are rating. Also, their job is made easier by the fact that most bonds are sold by firms with a track record of free cash flow to investors seeking relative safety and generally modest returns. Either the interest payments (sometimes called coupons) are paid or they aren't, so analysis tends to be focused on the margin of safety. Of course, every aspect of the firm's operations and financial results may have a bearing on

TABLE 9.1   BOND FUND COMPARISON

| | | % RANK WITHIN CATEGORY, 1=BEST, 100=WORST | | |
| | | 1 YEAR RETURN | 3 YEAR ANNUALIZED RETURN | 5 YEAR ANNUALIZED RETURN |
VANGUARD FUND	TICKER			
Vanguard Intermediate Bond Index	VBIIX	19	13	6
Vanguard Long-Term Bond Index	VBLTX	6	2	1
Vanguard Short-Term Bond Index	VBISX	20	10	8

SOURCE: Morningstar data as of 4/30/2002

this question, but not to the same extent as with the firm's stock, where wild swings in value can occur with small changes in revenues and earnings growth. Equity analysts are given the harder task of predicting these figures with relative precision.

The facts bear out indexing's strength in bonds, because the historical record offers plenty of evidence to prove the point. A review of active bond fund performance does not show remarkable deviation on average from index bond funds of comparable composition (see Table 9.1).

In light of the preceding discussion, why bother trying to outperform in this sector? Isn't safety what bonds are all about anyway? Active bond funds, like their equity kin, tend to concentrate their bets, so the chance of one bond greatly damaging the portfolio is greater than in a diversified index fund.

CHAPTER 10

Allocating Assets for Return and for Risk

At first, people laughed at the intrepid investors who were opting for "average performance." They considered it some-how un-American not to try harder."

—Peter L. Bernstein, *Capital Ideas*

Asset allocation is the key activity the index investor should focus on. As we saw in Chapter 6, research has demonstrated that the vast majority of performance by money managers can be explained by asset allocation, or the weighting of asset classes in a portfolio. Since the original Brinson study of 1986, it has been clear that more than 94% of portfolios' returns can be explained by asset class movement, completely aside from selection of an individual stock. That figure is likely to vary somewhat over time, but the importance of selecting asset classes carefully cannot be overstated.

Investors seem to spend most of their time and overall fees picking stocks (or paying someone to do it) and very little time deciding how to allocate assets generally. This should be turned on its head. Most of an investor's time should be spent allocating assets and very little considering individual securities. It's a more powerful version of the 80%–20% rule of life, which states that we spend 80% of our time on wasteful things and 20% on useful ones. Once stock picking is admitted to be wasteful, life for the investor is made easier.

Since indexers do not have to worry about stock picking, they can free up enormous time (if they do it themselves) or cash (if they pay a high annual fees to an active fund to do it for them). This is not to say that complete ignorance of individual company events is desirable. For background educational purposes, it is instructive to understand what makes individual companies tick so that one has a concrete understanding of what is inside indexes. Indexes of small-cap companies and international companies are different in nature than indexes of large-cap U.S. firms, because the economics and operations of the individual companies are so radically different in various environments. Then there are the lightning-rod companies, those firms that for whatever reason spur public debate over larger issues. The bankruptcy of Enron and the HP-Compaq merger fight illustrated something bigger about the state of companies and helped change policy by the government as well as behavior by millions of businesspersons. Often, veterinarians must conduct an in-depth medical examination of one animal to better understand the health of a herd, and following newsworthy companies such as Enron during its 2002 bankruptcy sheds light on business trends as a whole.

It seems to me most of the important asset class decisions are made when money is first invested, not during the occasional rebalancing or change in weighting that takes place later. I liken this to the old real estate adage: "You make your money on the way in, not on the way out." That is, selection of the property to purchase at the right time when future prospects are uncertain is where profits are made, and not at the time of sale when the assets' final value is clear.

Although there is a relevant and fairly easily identified average return within a homogeneous asset class, there is no such thing between such disparate asset classes as stocks and bonds. Indexing won't help you here! At its simplest, the two facets of an asset class under consideration are predicted return and risk. We all know that bonds provide generally safe returns and stocks provide generally higher returns with no guarantees. At one extreme end of this spectrum, short-term U.S. Treasury bonds generate a low, constant return with the assurance of the full backing of the U.S.

government. At the other end of the spectrum, small technology growth stocks provide absolutely no assurance that investors will ever see their money again, but there is the possibility of enormous appreciation.

For all the assets in the middle, degrees of risk and return may come in various combinations. Large-cap value companies generally carry dividends just like bonds, but they are somewhat risky—not as risky as small technology firms, but risky nonetheless. Risk is often described by its historical variation, and return is often described by historical annualized returns. As we have seen, everyone loves return and the financial media especially love to talk about return. Return is always the first thing mentioned about a fund. It is easy to calculate and is what all financial plans set as their primary goal. Risk should never be forgotten.

A few housekeeping items will help keep returns fair and accurate. Remember the Beardstown Ladies Investment Club mentioned earlier in this book? They thought they were far outperforming the market but in fact were not keeping clean records. Actual returns are the combination of stock appreciation and dividends, which are described as "total." Most investors simply reinvest the dividends, but some take them out. Just be aware and keep them separate.

In addition, be sure to use only returns that are net of all fees, including sales transaction costs. Remember that if there is a transaction cost at exit time (as with the exchange-traded funds we discuss later), this should be accounted for. Money taken out each year is no longer working for the investor. Generally, funds are required to state returns net of annual management fees.

Returns of multiple years may be quoted two ways: (1) as a simple average or (2) as compound annual growth rates of return, or simply annualized returns. Generally, returns are quoted as annualized because this allows returns from periods of different length to be compared with equivalent figures. Average data understates actual returns and penalizes longer periods. Most firms always quote annualized returns. This why we still find amusement from advertisements such as Lord Abbett's full-page *Wall Street Journal* spread on March 18, 2002, for various four and five-Morningstar-star funds (which means they were in the lofty top 32.5% of funds) touting various average performances. The firm was kind enough

TABLE 10.1
"STANDARDIZED" AVERAGE ANNUAL TOTAL

	1 YEAR	5 YEARS	TOTAL RETURN– 10 YEARS	10 YEARS OR SINCE INCEPTION
Lord Abbett MidCap Value Fund	1.79%	16.33%	150.70%	15.07%
Lord Abbett Affiliated Fund	–13.23%	10.84%	133.60%	13.36%
Lord Abbett Growth Opportunities Fund	–17.56%	13.21%	149.40%	14.94%
Lord Abbett All Value Fund	–9.72%	11.85%	142.90%	14.29%

"STANDARDIZED" ANNUALIZED RETURNS

	1 YEAR	5 YEARS	TOTAL RETURN– 5 YEARS	10 YEARS OR SINCE INCEPTION
Lord Abbett MidCap Value Fund	1.79%	16.28%	81.65%	14.97%
Lord Abbett Affiliated Fund	–13.23%	10.82%	54.20%	13.28%
Lord Abbett Growth Opportunities Fund	–17.56%	13.18%	66.05%	14.84%
Lord Abbett All Value Fund	–9.72%	11.82%	59.25%	14.20%

Formula for annualizing
   1) obtain total % return: (ending value/starting value)–1
   2) X = ((% return/100)+1)^1/(total # days/365)
   3) Annualized performance = (x–1)∗100

SOURCE: *Wall Street Journal* Ad, March 18, 2002

to include both average returns for various periods, as well as "standardized" average returns that account for its 5.75% sales load, but nowhere on the full-page ad could it squeeze in annualized returns. Table 10.1 translates the data to meaningful information.

Investors often find it useful to follow returns that are adjusted for inflation. These are called *real returns* and give a measure of true earning power. If an asset's return is 8% and inflation is 3%, the real return is 5%. During times of high inflation investors may seem as though they are getting rich, but in fact much of their earnings are being gobbled up by inflation. Also, a little common sense never hurts to assess the legitimacy of past returns. Most industries see periods of incubation, fast growth, and finally maturity. If the industry is technological in nature and subject to new inventions on a frequent basis, this process could happen in less than a decade. If the industry becomes a fundamental industrial sector, it is likely to take many decades.

"Double Check—Are your returns net of fees, annualized and inclusive of dividends?"

While everyone likes to talk about returns, no one seems to care much about risk. Journalists and analysts are generally not eager to talk about a company's risk before it crashes. (Is it lack of excitement and for fear of offending a potential customer?) Journalists do tend to perk up after the damage is done with plenty of articles about how to avoid the next crash and with sell recommendations for the stock that has already cratered.

Investors, too, tend to lag in their full appreciation of risk. A *Wall Street Journal*/NBC News poll in January, 2002, when investors had fully absorbed the impacts of recession and the September terrorist attack, showed that they felt markets were riskier and they felt less confident about how to proceed (See Table 10.2).[1]

These responses don't make sense. When a market falls hard, as a general rule there is less risk that it will fall so hard again. Reversion to the mean, proven over and over again throughout time, has shown that. It is

TABLE 10.2   RESPONSES OF 499 ADULTS IN A WSJ/NBC
                  NEWS POLL

HOW WOULD YOU RATE THE RISK OF LOSING MONEY IN THE STOCK MARKET TODAY COMPARED TO A YEAR AGO?	
Much or somewhat riskier:	53%
About as risky:	31%
Somewhat or much less risky:	15%
Not sure:	1%
COMPARED WITH A YEAR OR TWO AGO, WHEN IT COMES TO YOUR ABILITY TO MANAGE YOUR INVESTING ACTIVITIES TODAY, HOW CONFIDENT WOULD YOU SAY YOU ARE?	
Much or somewhat more confident:	20%
As confident:	47%
Somewhat or much less confident:	32%
Not sure:	1%
DO YOU THINK THAT YOU WILL OR WILL NOT TURN TO A PROFESSIONAL FOR INVESTING ASSISTANCE IN THE COMING YEAR?	
Yes, will turn to a professional:	48%
No, will not turn to a professional:	50%
Not sure:	2%

SOURCE: "Investors Rate the Market's Risks," *The Wall Street Journal*, January 2002

precisely when things are going well, risk is perceived to be low, and (most importantly) valuations have been bid up that the risk is highest.

A little housekeeping with risk, too, may help keep terminology straight. Risk is generally described as a statistical measure called a standard deviation in variation of prices. If a return is certain, it is low risk, but if it jumps up and down, it is clearly high risk. It so happens in natural phenomena that data of growth and change generally falls into a nice, bell-shaped curve. This includes most economic activity, since it is driven by the relatively random activity of human beings. Conveniently, this tends to produce a standard measure of variation called a *standard deviation*. Simply put, any outcome greater than one standard deviation from the mean or average return is expected to occur about one-third of the time, any outcome greater than two standard deviations is predicted to occur no more than

FIGURE 10.1   BELL-SHAPED CURVE OF RETURNS

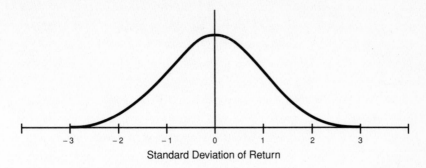

Standard Deviation of Return

about 5% of the time, and any outcome greater than three standard deviations is expected to occur less than about 1% of the time (see Figure 10.1).

The deviation can be negative or positive. The amount of data and
the length of time behind the prediction are indicators of the strength of
the prediction. A standard deviation built on only 60 days of data should
be greeted with some skepticism, while one built on 600 days of data
should be given greater credence.

Standard deviations for funds and indexes are found in many reports,
and since the unit of risk is standardized, it is easy to compare financial
entities. For most index funds, you may find this and other statistics in the
data area of IndexFunds.com. Just look up the standard deviation and ask
yourself, "Am I concerned that there is a one-third chance that this fund or
index will decline in price by this amount (one standard deviation) over the
next year?" The same can be done with two and three standard deviations.

Standard deviations can be compared between asset classes to get a
sense of which ones jump around and which ones tend to be stable.
Common sense should be used here as well. Risk that has been muted for
years can break out all of a sudden.

It needs to be stressed that all "expected" or "anticipated" returns and
risks for equities are just guesses. Typically, these guesses are arrived at
with historical figures, estimates from analysts, or simply commonsense
hunches by investors and their advisors. As Stanford Professor William
Sharpe put it, "Most performance measures are computed using historic
data but justified on the basis of predicted relationships."[2]

All relevant factors have their place. The indexing industry has a tendency to engage in pure number crunching without sufficient consideration of economic context. Indexers are often great fans of facts and figures, given their skepticism of the subjective stock-picking acumen of money managers. However, at times this drives them to be too concerned with historical numbers.

Financial models operate very much under the "garbage-in-garbage-out" effect. It is important to view assumptions underpinning the models with a critical eye. I favor an approach that encourages judgment and common sense. Investors should ask themselves questions such as:

- What would likely happen with various outcomes?

- Do I really believe these projected rates of growth and inflation?

- Do these figures agree with longer-term historical data?

As we saw previously, data mining of historical information is a self-serving but often impressive use of number crunching that needs to be guarded against. When examining the return of an asset class (or for that matter of an associated index or actual index fund), remember that it is important to examine a variety of periods during which performance is assessed. One of the most obvious misuses of comparative time periods is when returns for U.S. equities are quoted for the period just after the severe 1973–1974 recession. This convenient selection of dates can make a difference of 40% for some asset classes. Likewise, any analysis starting in 1988 conveniently misses the short but pronounced October 1987 crash that sent stocks reeling.

Remember that the great leveler discussed in Chapter 6, reversion to the mean, tends to flatten out or reverse historical trends. Furthermore, there are rare historical discontinuities that have profound effects. Even though equity investors have had a string of decades with excellent returns, an event that decimates stocks like the Great Depression can happen at any time. In today's market, equity investors have the war on terrorism to consider.

The Al Qaeda and other networks have all but said they would use any destructive device at their means against the United States. Pentagon officials have publicly warned against the possibility of TNT laced with uranium that could render an urban center uninhabitable. What would that do to U.S. stocks? No doubt it would punish them severely.

Some major risks loom large over markets, and even if you believe that markets have incorporated all risks into prices, that still doesn't mean the risk is appropriate for the individual investor. The point is that cataclysmic financial events can occur on the heels of a half-century or more of relative stability.

Return and risk are often best analyzed together and should never be too far apart during any sensible discussion of investment. Who wants to invest their entire portfolio in a stock that has shot up during the last year if in the view of reasonable people it may well be bankrupt during the next? Assets that show higher returns over time with equal risk tend to attract more capital, and the reverse also is true. But looking back into history there certainly are periods where high-risk assets, as judged by their high standard deviations, produce low return. Figure 10.2 shows such a case for US equity classes for the 20-year period leading up to 4/30/2002.

FIGURE 10.2   RISK AND RETURN OF 10 MAJOR INDEX CATEGORIES

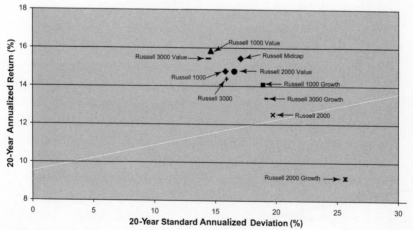

SOURCE: Morningstar data as of 4/30/2002

Over time, higher returns appear from the following asset classes:

- Smaller companies

- International companies

- Value (low-growth) companies

Most of this extra return compared to large U.S. companies is attributed to additional risk and is often called the *size risk premium*. However, there is debate about whether value companies may consistently deliver higher return at lower risk than growth funds. The general rule of thumb is that extra return carries extra risk. In hindsight, there are always markets that turn out to be more stable and more rewarding than previously thought. But it is rare to see an asset class to carry lower risk at higher return.

A very useful measure of risk-adjusted return, called the Sharpe Ratio, helps compare a fund to a benchmark index or asset class. Named for Stanford Professor William Sharpe, it unites mean returns (performance) with variance (risk). It requires that the difference in expected returns between the fund and its benchmark be known. The benchmark can be as simple as a riskless asset such as Treasury bills. If used with historical data, it can be expressed in the following way:

$$\text{Sharpe Ratio} = \frac{\text{Expected Differential Return}}{\text{Predicted Standard Deviation}}$$

A bigger Sharpe Ratio is better, all else being equal. The proper use of the Sharpe requires some care: "When choosing one from among a set of funds to provide representation in a particular market sector, it makes sense to favor the one with the greatest predicted Sharpe Ratio, as long as the correlations of the funds with other relevant asset classes are reasonably similar. When allocating funds among several such funds, it makes sense to allocate funds such that the selection (residual) risk levels are proportional to the predicted Sharpe Ratios for the selection (residual) returns. If some of the implied net positions are infeasible or involve excessive transactions costs, of course, the decision rules must be modified. Nonetheless, Sharpe Ratios may still provide useful guidance, according to Professor Sharpe."[3]

The surest way to beat the "average" performance is to choose riskier assets. Thus, money managers often beat an index because they invest in assets that are riskier. We saw earlier how Peter Lynch admits to it fully in regard to Fidelity Magellan's success, and how the professionals in *The Wall Street Journal* competition actually underperformed the dartboard, after risks were taken into consideration (See Table 10.3).

When combining multiple asset classes into a portfolio, how they correlate also comes into play. Ultimately, it's the total volatility of the portfolio that interests the investor. Just selecting asset classes that individually seem the most stable is not necessarily going to lead to the lowest total volatility. If for instance, two highly volatile asset classes are

TABLE 10.3   RETURNS AND VOLATILITY OF MAJOR ASSET
             CLASSES

INDEX NAME	20-YR STANDARD DEVIATION	20-YEAR ANNUALIZED RETURN
Lehman Brothers Aggregate Bond	4.98	10.56
Salomon Brothers Treasury	5.06	10.03
MSCI EAFE Equity Index	17.74	11.62
Russell 1000	15.82	15.17
Russell 1000 Growth	18.90	14.10
Russell 1000 Value	14.56	15.83
Russell 2000	20.21	12.24
Russell 2000 Growth	25.15	8.89
Russell 2000 Value	16.55	15.16
Russell 3000	15.91	14.88
Russell 3000 Growth Index	19.13	13.50
Russell 3000 Value Index	14.47	15.73
Russell Midcap Index	17.06	15.38

SOURCE: Wiesenberger data as of 2/28/02

perfectly uncorrelated, they will in fact combine to make a less risky portfolio than two low-volatility asset classes that move together (Table 10.4 and Figure 10.3).

When combining multiple asset classes, keeping track of all the correlations and their effects becomes cumbersome, so a nice short cut is delivered with a market correlation, often described as *beta*. A high correlation with the overall market or beta does nothing to dampen portfolio volatility, whereas a low or the more unusual negative beta does and therefore makes an asset class more valuable, all else being equal. It is sometimes hard to predict the optimal balance of multiple assets, but there is an optimal combination of assets to produce the highest return for each level of overall risk. This is called the *efficient frontier*. It usually turns out to be a convex curve when drawn against a figure of risk versus return (see Figure 10.4).

As an investor, you want to be close to the edge of the curve. If you are picking combinations that do not lie on the curve, you have not done your homework from a theoretical point of view. There are combinations that will provide higher returns with no more risk (as judged by historical data) or lower risk at the same return.

To some observers, time is almost as important as risk and return. This is because stocks appear "less risky" the longer the time period considered.

TABLE 10.4   WHEN COMBINED, VOLATILE BUT
             UNCORRELATED ASSETS CAN PRODUCE
             A LESS RISKY PORTFOLIO

| | 4-YEAR TIME PERIOD | | | |
| | 1 | 2 | 3 | 4 |
ASSETS	RETURN DURING TIME PERIOD (%)			
A	3	−3	3	−3
B	−2	2	−2	2
A+B Portfolio	1	−1	1	−1
C	2	−2	2	−2
D	1	−1	1	−1
C+D Portfolio	3	−3	3	−3

FIGURE 10.3   ASSETS A AND B ARE VOLATILE BUT
                 TOGETHER MAKE A STABLE PORTFOLIO

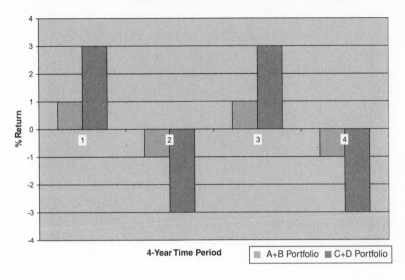

FIGURE 10.4   RISK AND RETURN OF VARIOUS INDEXES

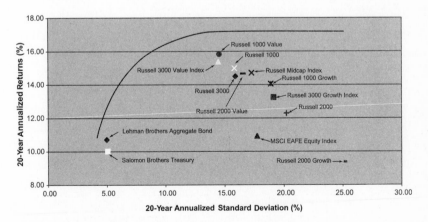

The hand-drawn curve appoximates portfolios with the highest returns for the lowest risk.
SOURCE: Morningstar data as of 4/30/2002

Everyone knows that stocks are risky and bonds give low returns. However, such comparisons are generally over a one-year time frame. If you lengthen the period, stocks not only have greater returns on average, they actually more consistently come up positive. True, they may stumble badly, but they can be more sure of outpacing bonds during a long investment period. This is seen in historical returns for this century no matter how you look at the data (See Figure 2.1 on page 16).

I caution against allowing this concept, which is nonetheless well founded, from blinding the investor to common sense and prudence. Taken to its extreme, we should all hold the view that stocks are only slightly more risky than bonds, or as 1998 Nobel Prize-winning economist Paul Samuelson put it: "Many people now believe that if they simply hold stocks long enough they will not lose money for statistics have shown that since 1926 the U.S. equity market has not suffered a loss in any given 15 years." His answer to this way of thinking is that "Risk does not go to zero over long periods."[4]

Furthermore, as investors have come to depend on the long-term supremacy of stocks, they shift more and more assets into stocks. The added return from owning stocks, or the risk premium, has shrunk from previous decades, many economists believe. If this is true, the dual result will be that stocks will not outstrip bonds so easily and will show less safety over short- and long-term periods. Samuelson notes that as: "More and more people recognize the statistical long-term trend in stock returns and invest accordingly, it is going to raise the price to earnings ratio of the marketplace. As to just how high it can go before becoming irrational, nobody knows. But looking at where Japan is today might give you a good idea of what euphoria and perceived unlimited growth to the future can portend."[5]

Stocks can crash, sometimes severely and for years on end. It is best if the investor confronts this as a real possibility. There seem to be two forms of stock market crashes. One is essentially a correction, admittedly sharp at times, of high valuations. I put the crash of 1987 in that category. Even though stocks dipped by more than 20%, they also bounced back within a year. Another kind of crash also involves an underlying economic malaise. The debilitating recession of 1973 to 1974 grew out of oil embargoes, the costly Vietnam War, and rising inflation. The crash of 1929 was followed by Depression, not because stocks were expensive but because the banks failed. The credit system was clearly faulty.

The investor must ask this question at all times: Is there some systematic illness present or lurking in the economy or society? I believe the main risk of debilitating loss for U.S. equity investors is the prospect of war between Western and radical cultures should rogue states continue to sponsor terrorism brazenly.

Prior to September 11, it was inconceivable that any fringe group would be able to bring a major financial market to its knees, either for a day or for a week. Not so any more. Now the stakes are even higher, as it is clear that terrorists will seek to obtain weapons of mass destruction. The war on terrorism and the degree of carnage suffered in the process is impossible to predict, and prudent investors can only follow their hunches in charting a course for themselves. Such concern is not a matter of patriotism or ideology, but rather a fundamental matter of economics. A straightforward assessment and acknowledgement of actual risks is the best policy for allocating resources for the individual and for nations as a whole.

THE NEW MILLENNIUM QUANDARY

Now for the main quandary faced by investors as they enter 2003. A consensus of the most perceptive economists and advisors is asking the following question: Can the economy grow sufficiently fast to earn its way out of current high stock prices? Even after 3 years of dismal drops for most indexes, equities are at historically high valuation levels, no matter what metric you use. Some observers like to focus on financial statement earnings, others like to focus on free cash flow and still others on book value.

Over time, a nation's equities have followed the path of the economy, despite surges and lags. If you believe that the economy will grow at similar levels as found in the past, then you should concede that stock returns will be low on average in coming years until these metrics improve.

If, on the other hand, you feel the economy will pick up quickly again and resume above-average growth rates, then it is feasible that today's equity prices are fairly priced to reflect tomorrow's excellent earnings, cash flow or net asset value. No one can make predictions, but investors should be aware that a substantial number of economists, analysts, and investors do not believe in the prospects of sustained above-average growth and therefore predict dampened stock returns for years to come. Warren Buffett is one such person.

The main thing holding many investors back is low interest rates and the resultant low yields on bonds. Investors seem to have concluded that stocks are risky but bonds don't give sufficient return. Should interest rates rise and bond yields climb without a pickup in corporate earnings growth, look out, stocks! No one has a crystal ball, but everyone has to answer this quandary in their own way. I personally side with the skeptical crowd that feels growth will continue at a steady pace, but not far above historical norms, and will not bail out stocks from their high valuations. Therefore returns will be modest in years to come. Stocks are still the investment of choice, but occasional defensive postures based on common sense may be more necessary in today's climate. On the other hand, I also believe the most advanced economies will continue to leverage computers and modern management techniques to drive continuous improvements in valuable new products and services.

Of course, there is no magic formula for solving the problem, but awareness and education will certainly help. Books such as *Valuing Wall Street*, which explains various methodologies for predicting excessive risk, are of particular value in today's climate. Its authors claim the book "doesn't preach that stocks are dangerous. Quite the opposite: It reassures us that a long-range investor should be heavily invested in stocks—most of the time. But it also reminds that, during certain periods in history, stocks can be so overvalued that they are entirely the wrong place to be."[6]

An indexing philosophy based on common sense and judgment, in my view, will help shield investors from the very worst falls. The infrequent crashes that really hammer a portfolio for more than a year inevitably come in markets that most knowledgeable individuals versed in a little bit of financial history would say are frothy and speculative. In my view, the rules of the game in this era of generally frothy valuations have changed slightly. Although a pure stock portfolio with an unbending buy-and-hold philosophy did wonders in recent decades, that is less likely to hold true given today's generally high valuations.

Normally at IndexFunds.com we recommend maintaining steady allocation percentages over time, but we also endorse common-sense exceptions to this rule on occasion. At its simplest, the opportunistic indexer can rotate 10% to 30% (or more) of a portfolio from stocks to bonds (and back again later) as the market becomes frothy.

CHAPTER 11

Asset Classes

Asset classes come in many flavors and can be as different in nature as night and day. Stocks, bonds, and real estate are general asset classes, whereas U.S. small-cap value is one of the more precise ones. As the investor zeroes in on attractive asset classes, it is useful to consider their features at a particular point in time. Asset classes vary in nature over the short-term and mutate fairly significantly over longer stretches as well.

Enterprising researchers have gathered records for equity returns in the United States well into the early 1800s and far earlier than that in Europe. I am not sure that the growth of primarily agricultural economies is directly comparable to modern industrial ones, but the curious result of this research is that not too much has changed. One study found total real returns (total returns less inflation) of 7% from 1980 to 1997 with huge run-ups and drastic crashes found in every era. The main aspect of the last three decades of investment appears to be higher inflation coupled with historically very high returns that resulted in above-average real returns.[1]

As we enter the new millennium, we are coming off one of the great contests between large companies and small and between growth and value (see Figure 11.1). It is unusual because in most decades small stocks win. This time growth stocks and large caps shot up as the telecom and Internet bubble took off.

As the decade ended, the bubble was bursting and growth stocks especially but also larges cap generally took a big hit.

Clearly, as we close out 2002 we are back to a more even playing field, where it's harder to argue that one asset class is clearly overvalued compared to another. If anything, they may *all* be overvalued. Probably the largest chorus of predictions is that small-cap stocks, and especially value stocks, are expected by some to recoup some more of their previous lag.

FIGURE 11.1   LARGE CAPS VERSUS SMALL CAPS IN 1990s
AND 2001

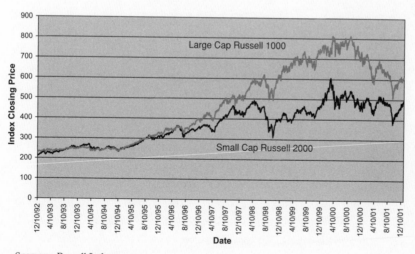

SOURCE: Russell Indexes

FIGURE 11.2   MAJOR ASSET CLASSES ACROSS TIME 1995–2002

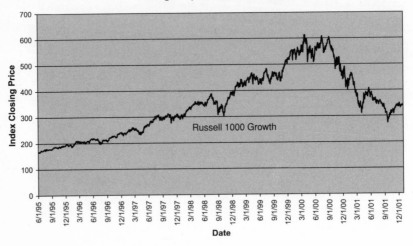

Large Cap Growth - 1995-2002

SOURCE: Russell Indexes

U.S. LARGE CAPS

Large caps or companies whose market capitalizations are large should be in every portfolio because they represent such a large percentage of economic activity. For instance, in the late 1990s the technology bubble (see Figure 11.2) caused the U.S. large-cap asset class (and resulting indexes such as the S&P 500) to be dominated by technology growth stocks (see Table 11.1).

In that sense it made little sense to speak about large caps over two decades as if it they were the same creature. Now the S&P is much more consistent with what it was in the 1980s and 1970s, a grab bag of industrial behemoths with a sprinkling of technology.

As in biology, nothing stays exactly the same in finance. Investments are like species that mutate, and their environment or ecology changes, expands, and contracts. So, too, asset classes change over time. A stock is not a stock is not a stock. Its fundamental nature will change in relation to the investor over time.

TABLE 11.1   PERCENTAGE OF S&P 500 IN TECHNOLOGY
STOCKS RISE AND THEN FALL

DATE	% OF S&P 500 IN TECHNOLOGY
12/25/95	11.92
12/31/96	14.79
12/31/97	14.45
12/31/98	19.01
12/31/99	28.22
12/31/00	22.63
12/31/01	18.94%

SOURCE: Barra.com

U.S. MID CAPS

Over the past three decades mid-cap stocks have shown some of the extra upside of small-cap stocks with less of the volatility. They remain the obvious first asset class to branch out to beyond large caps. A curious phenomenon occurred during the latter part of the 1990s. With small-cap stocks lagging so badly and large-cap stocks shooting up in valuation, the range of valuation that defines a mid-cap stock grew from about $1 billion to just over $4 billion in 1994 to $1 billion to over $8 billion in 2002.[2]

Not everyone likes the mid-cap asset class when it is actually used in a portfolio. Advisor Larry Swedroe points out that mid caps are a perfectly fine asset class per se. The problem is that they, in conjunction with large- and small-cap asset classes, correlate with large caps far more than small caps. Thus, he argues, ". . . if investors are going to own the large-cap asset class as part of their portfolio, the most effective diversifier is the very smallest of the small-cap stocks. When constructing a portfolio, the goal is to add low-correlating asset classes to reduce portfolio volatility."

This is a classic use of thoughtful portfolio construction. Owning more of each of these two extreme classes may on average provide a little better return with a little lower risk. This is not always the case, but the numbers suggest it is plausible. Mid-cap funds have higher fees and turnover costs and can be expected to distribute higher capital gains than large-cap funds.

U.S. SMALL CAPS

The small-cap asset class is where investors go to get an extra pop in the stock market, but watch out! They are more volatile. As the asset class that was left farthest in the dust during the late 1990s, small-cap stocks were perhaps the ones with the best chance of a rebound and showed strength in 2002. This is suggested by their long-term strength and by the tendency of returns to revert to the mean.

Not only are small-cap stocks volatile as a group, their internal components are volatile as well. Consider that in the first quarter of 2002 small-cap value stocks were the best performing major asset class and small-cap growth stocks were worst.[3] One of the strange anomalies of small-cap

FIGURE 11.3   SMALL CAP GROWTH AND VALUE IN
                LATE 1990S

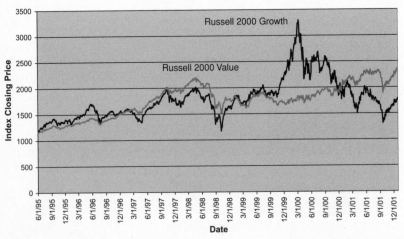

SOURCE: Russell Indexes

stocks is that their growth half (usually described as the half with the highest price-to-earnings ratio) slightly lags the value half over most recent time periods *and* shows significantly higher volatility, or the worst of both worlds (see Figure 11.3).

One explanation for this is that when successful small technology companies rocket out of the small-cap arena, much of the benefit is captured by the mid-cap asset class as they continue to expand. At the same time, losers falling out of mid-cap status tend to sink and finally go bankrupt while within the small-cap arena. Thus, the small-cap asset class benefits only partially from the winners and more fully from the losers. If you like small caps, then beware of their growth side.

Small-cap stocks get a bad rap because of the high turnover from some indexes built around them. Yes, they do tend to fly in and out of indexes. However, that is not a trait of the asset class per se, and there are passive strategies that can keep turnover to a minimum, as we shall see in Chapter 15.

GROWTH STOCKS

No sector elicited more excitement and then more disgust in the last decade than growth stocks, whether they be large, medium, small, or international. Growth stocks are generally defined as those that are perceived to be growing earnings or cash flow at a faster rate than others. In most environments, investors will pay significantly more per dollar of current earnings for such stocks, so their prices have such expectations built into them. Because no one can predict how earnings truly will grow, they can go down sharply if their prospects become more mundane all of a sudden. This does not mean that a portfolio of growth stocks is likely to "grow" faster than a value portfolio. If anything, much of the historical data suggests that growth has been riskier while performing more poorly than value.

The degree to which an asset class is considered a "growth" type is often described by its price-to-earnings (P/E) ratio, or the multiple paid for one year of recent earnings. Investors paying 100 times last year's earnings when the average is 30 are clearly hoping that earnings will continue to rise so in a few years they will have paid less than the market average and still look forward to more catching up (see Table 11.2). Normally growth refers to the half of an asset class's companies with the highest P/E ratios.

Price-to-earnings ratios have their critics. A company generating particularly good earnings due to a series of unusual events could see its P/E plummet, making it seem less of a growth stock than it probably is. Likewise, a firm generating consistent earnings but having a poor year could see its P/E skyrocket, putting it into the growth category. Remember, if earnings go up, the P/E ratio will fall, and if earnings decline, the P/E ratio will rise, assuming that price remains stable. What to make of the firm that posts a loss? It happens to the best of firms, but for the person glued to the P/E, the ratio is negative. Over time, of course, prices will rise or fall in reaction to earnings changes, but in the meantime very strange P/E ratios can pop up and confound the eager number cruncher.

TABLE 11.2   1-YEAR TRADING PRICE-TO-EARNINGS RATIO OF VARIOUS POPULAR INDEXES

INDEX	P/E RATIO
Russell 1000 (Large Cap)	30.6
Russell 1000 Growth	37.1
Russell 1000 Value	25.4
Russell 2000 (Small Cap)	25.2
Russell 2000 Growth	29.1
Russell 2000 Value	22.6
Russell 3000 (Total Market)	30.3
Russell Midcap	28.8
Russell Midcap Growth	36.7
Russell Midcap Value	24.1
Standard & Poor's 500 (Large Cap)	31.9
Standard & Poor's Midcap 400	28.8
Standard & Poor's Smallcap 600	27.6

SOURCE: Morningstar data as of 4/30/2002

Another candidate for determining a growth stock is the price-to-book value ratio, or its inverse, book value-to-price. Book value is the accounting net worth of a firm were it to be liquidated. It's considered by many a stable indicator of true economic value. Perhaps the least followed but most reliable valuation is price-to-cash flow. It is hard to fudge cash flow.

It is clear to most observers (but of little use to investors now) that the surge in growth in the 1990s was largely speculative, or "irrational exuberance," as Federal Reserve Chairman Alan Greenspan put it well before it hit its peak. Many still await further underperformance relative to value, and as was mentioned in the last chapter, this will probably hinge on the degree of growth spurred by technology.

VALUE STOCKS

Anyone who fears the growth asset class necessarily seeks the value asset class, and as was suggested by the previous section on growth stocks, it may be the smart play. In style indexes, the value component contains companies within the asset class that have lower P/E or other valuation measures. This group has shown far less susceptibility to turbulence and overvaluation than growth stocks, and during most comparison periods has ground out a better return overall in recent decades. Many leading advisors favor value stocks heavily. As mentioned in the chapter on theory of indexing, there is intriguing data supporting many of their contentions. Keep in mind that growth stocks plummeted in 2000 to 2002, and that the value asset class has come back into balance in recent years and does not offer quite so obvious a bargain next to growth.

SECTORS

Sectors are groups of stocks that represent individual industries. In the view of IndexFunds.com, investing in sectors should be kept to less than 10% of a portfolio for most investors. If one is thoroughly familiar with asset allocation and has performed all the steps outlined in Part II of this book, then it may be appropriate. Keep in mind that sector funds are more expensive, but new offerings are bringing costs down. One of the best reasons to bet on a particular sector is if one has particular insight, knowledge, and experience with an industry. Typically, that comes with being employed in it or living in an area where it is pervasive. Unfortunately, that endangers the investor by increasing their exposure to that industry. It's one thing to lose one's job because of an industry downturn, but it is entirely another to also take a hit to one's portfolio from that downturn at the same time.

INTERNATIONAL

International stocks lend themselves very well to indexing, which surprises some investors. The key is to sidestep poor markets using common sense. Most Japanese stocks in the late 1980s were a good example, and US tech stocks in the 1990s were another of stocks that were fairly obviously overvalued.

International funds have long been a favorite method of lowering overall portfolio volatility, because in the past stocks from one region of the world have not correlated highly with those of another. This is no longer the case. The decade of the 1990s saw further intermeshing of economies as globalization took hold with a vengeance, regardless of how many protesters took to the streets against it. Princeton economist William Baumol believes that productivity figures for modern economies shows convergence. The difference between very productive nations and formerly less unproductive ones has narrowed. Indeed, trends in the markets show convergence of correlations, as shown in Figure 11.4.

It turns out that this is not a new phenomenon. Research from Michael Bordo, an economist at Rutgers University, shows that between 1893 and 1945, there was more correlation between major industrial nations than after the World War II.[4] Apparently, we are returning to a harmonized world economy. How could it be otherwise in the new global economy? National giants had to go beyond their own markets to continue to expand, and communications costs have dropped from technological innovation.

FIGURE 11.4   U.S. VERSUS INTERNATIONAL STOCKS,
                   1997–2002, R-SQUARED CORRELATION = 0.66

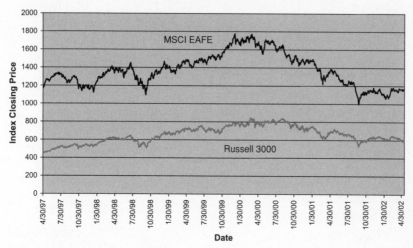

SOURCE: Russell Indexes and Reuters

The main problem with international stocks is the cost of international custody and currency exchange.

BONDS

Bonds are the great refuge from the vagaries of the stock market. Unfortunately, their returns are now quite low, and as always, their dividends are taxable at regular federal and state income rates, which can exceed 40% for high-income investors. Indexing with bonds is perhaps more compelling a strategy than indexing with equities. The fact is that rating agencies have a fairly reliable risk ratings so that a well-diversified bond index fund is not going to vary much from active funds. For investment-grade bonds (as opposed to more speculative high-yield or "junk" bonds), there just isn't that much room to outperform the market, whether through luck or skill (consider the plot of intermediate-term bond funds in Table 11.3), and saving every penny when returns are low to begin with is especially important.

TABLE 11.3   BOND STANDARD DEVIATION FOR 2001

INDEX	STD DEV 3 YR	STD DEV 5 YR	STD DEV 10 YR
Lehman Brothers Intermediate Credit	3.40	3.47	4.06
Lehman Brothers Intermediate Government Bond	3.12	3.03	3.33
Lehman Brothers Intermediate Government/Credit	3.13	3.06	3.33
Lehman Brothers Intermediate Treasury	3.01	3.00	3.25
S&P 500	**16.06**	**19.32**	**15.92**

SOURCE: Morningstar data as of 4/30/2002

Long-term bonds seem tempting for the new investor. Why would someone pass up higher interest from long-term bonds to settle for lower interest from short-term ones? The answer is because they are risky and their risk correlates relatively highly with equities. Long-term bonds currently lock in investor to low rates for very long periods of time, so any sharp rise in interest rates will drop their intrinsic value. Also, long-term bonds correlate more with the market returns, so they don't add useful diversification in the same way as short-term bonds. At this point in time, the argument is especially strong. With interest rates so low, long-term bonds now have a reasonably high chance of tumbling in value more than at any time in decades. Short-term bonds and perhaps a dabbling of three- to five-year bonds are most recommended.

CHAPTER 12

Fees Are Not
Your Friend

*From much of that I hear, I am known as a sort of fringe—
an apostle of the message that costs play a crucial role in
shaping long-term fund returns.*

—John Bogle, *Common Sense on Mutual Funds*

Throughout this book, we describe fees as the most important reason why index funds outpace active ones. Numerous studies have confirmed this result. This chapter looks a little deeper into this important subject. Doing so makes it much more clear how and why fees are not the friend of the investor. Fees remain extremely high, well over 1% for many asset classes (see Table 12.1).

It should be noted that large-cap fund fees should be lower than small-cap fund fees, and these in turn should be lower than international fund fees. There is more work involved with chasing down lots of small stocks, and with international funds there are substantial additional management costs, including special custodial holding of stocks across borders, hedging of currency, and travel to various parts of the world.

One thing that amazes us is that fees have not come down as a result of competition among funds. There has been a huge expansion in the number of funds, from about 1200 domestic stock funds in 1991 to about

4800 in 2002, but this has not led to a drop in fees over time. They are still just about as high as the market can possibly bear. Competition in the active mutual fund industry has not involved price competition. This actually makes sense if consumers only are interested in one feature: "superior" performance. If mutual funds can't gather more customers by dropping fees, then why should they bother? Fees are paid for services that are presumed to be worth more in investment performance than their cost. Thus, there is a utility curve that probably is shaped something like the one shown in Figure 12.1. The exact shape of this curve in the real world is anyone's guess.

In Figure 12.1 fees are assumed to be at least 0.1% of assets per year, as this appears to be the bare minimum any investor, whether a giant institution or a small investor, can get away with. A minimum level of financial fees is unavoidable, a certain amount more is money well spent, and beyond that modest amount, we say the utility is doubtful. How quickly that curve turns upwards is the issue.

What are the penalties for spending too much on financial services? For long-term investments a penny saved on fees is truly a penny earned, many times over, because of the truly phenomenal power of compounding

TABLE 12.1   FEES BROKEN DOWN BY ASSET CLASS

FUND CATEGORY	AVERAGE EXPENSE RATIO
Large Blend	1.23%
Large Growth	1.46%
Large Value	1.41%
Mid-Cap Blend	1.41%
Mid-Cap Growth	1.53%
Mid-Cap Value	1.44%
Small Blend	1.44%
Small Growth	1.61%
Small Value	1.51%

SOURCE: Morningstar data as of 1/14/2002

FIGURE 12.1   INVESTORS PROFIT FROM SOME BUT NOT TOO
MANY FINANCIAL SERVICES

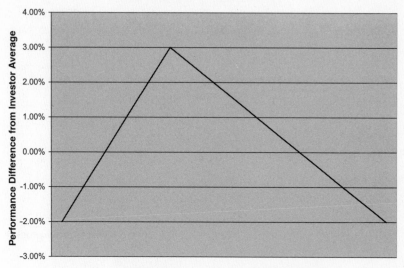

Annual Percentage Fees for Financial Services
Expenditure as a % of Total Assets per Year

interest. Compounding interest grows any amount of money over time. Where fees are concerned, the investors can choose whether to allow them to grow in their own account or in the accounts of their brokers or money managers. This is knowledge that any competent investors carry around with them to combat the onslaught of financial media noise and Wall Street marketing gloss.

The key figure indexers watch is the relative difference they can make with low-fee funds versus high-fee ones (see Figure 12.2).

As a rule of thumb for stocks returning around 10% per year, paying another 1% in extra fees means having to wait about two years more every decade for your portfolio to double. The astounding effect on actual returns by fund management fees can be graphed as shown in Figure 12.3.

Clearly, in a competitive environment, high fees make it really hard to beat the averages. It is no surprise that every reputable study of fund performance has found that high fees are the number one predictor of underperformance. This includes studies by Malkiel, Sharpe, and many others.

FIGURE 12.2   HOW SAVED FEES GROW OVER TIME—HOW
MUCH MORE YOUR FUND WILL BE WORTH IF
YOU REDUCE FEES BY 1%

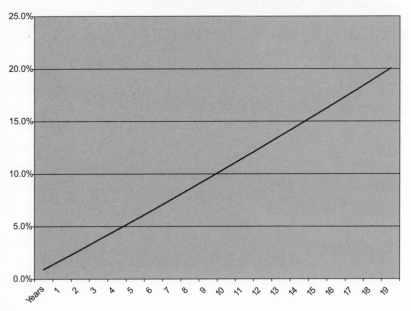

Nor is there any evidence that whether exceptional managerial performance in the past will continue and therefore is worth the extra costs. You know our view, and in previous chapters you have seen the evidence.

If there is a nice bell-shaped curve of returns, as we would expect in any natural phenomena, then it's a good bet to conclude that random factors govern the market. Fees, of course, simply lower the net return for the investor. Their rates are decided individually by each fund, and your willingness to pay high rates is decided individually by you!

If the data was skewed, we might have to reconsider. Well, the data comes in just as predicted.

We see the nice, bell-shaped curve, with most funds bunched around the average with a few stars to the right and real losers to the left (see Figure 6.1 on page 56). Rolling dice, the quintessential natural phenomena that defines luck, would give you just about the same curve, much like the one shown in Figure 10.1 on page 105.

Another way to look at the issue of expenses is to tally up the total amount of money spent in the industry and ask, "What is it all for?" We did just that at IndexFunds.com with a tool we called the *waste meter*. It tallied up how much more investors pay for mutual funds above and beyond fees of low-cost index offerings. It came to an astounding $36 billion in 2000.

This tool meticulously counted actual total fees charged by funds. It broke down over 8500 funds into 41 different investment categories. Only retail active and index funds were tracked, so the actual amount would be much higher if it included institutional investors, and sales commissions and transaction fees for buying funds were not factored in. For each category, a low-fee benchmark fund that most closely correlated with the fund was selected. (Admittedly, many funds wander off into their own "asset class." What they represent is often hard to tell.) The study then examined each of 8545 individual mutual funds, subtracting the total expense ratio of the category benchmark from the fund's total expense ratio. The excess expense ratio was multiplied by the fund's total net assets to arrive

FIGURE 12.3   **HOW AN EXTRA 1% IN SAVED FEES GROWS**

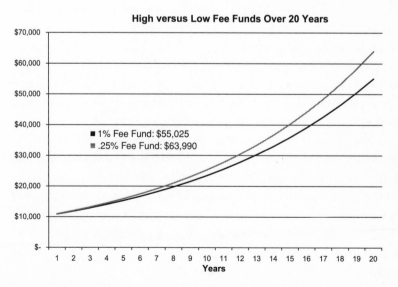

High versus Low Fee Funds Over 20 Years

■ 1% Fee Fund: $55,025
▪ .25% Fee Fund: $63,990

at the total excess fees paid annually by investors in that fund. The sum for all funds indicates the degree of waste present on Wall Street. Naturally, not all investors can index. Someone has to keep the markets competitive, so we were not claiming that all $36 billion was recoverable. But surely some of it was. Is there really a need to spend that much money in non-productive behavior?

It is curious that only a tiny minority of funds charge fees based on performance. They collect their 1% to 2% regardless of whether they out-perform their benchmark or return a profit at all. The hedge fund indus-try gets the best of both worlds; typically these speculative funds charge 1% of assets plus 20% of profits. Now that is a compensation package that hedges its bets!

When the returns of stocks are high, a high fee is noticed less. Inves-tors will still come out substantially ahead in absolute numbers, even if they could have had more. However, in today's environment of low expected stock appreciation, high fees are really a foot to the brake pedal. Consider that 1% fees paid out when stocks are accumulating 14% per year are only a 7% drag on returns, whereas 1% fees paid out when stocks are limping along with 8% returns translate into a 12.5% drag on returns. The fee hasn't changed, but its relation to the rest of the world has. All of a sudden, it's a very noticeable impediment to wealth accumulation.

Every fund, whether active or index, has annual fees. It must pay accountants, buy computers, fill out endless government paperwork, and answer questions from its investors (much of this is outsourced, but it still costs money). Fee types typically include management fees, marketing or 12b-1 fees, transaction costs, and sales commissions. The first three are normally extracted on an annual basis, whereas sales commissions are nor-mally paid up front or upon redemption.

Management fees are unavoidable. A handful of expert analysts need to be hired to track the portfolio, guided by an individual with experience. In an index fund the team can be as small as a few individuals, and in big active funds it can be a dozen or more. These costs are fairly fixed and rel-atively independent of fund's size. Then there are a slew of custodial, dis-tribution, and customer service fees. By law these roles are separated to keep a system of checks and balances in place so that assets are guarded closely. Any activity having to do with customer service is dependent on the number of customers, so total costs will rise along with that number, but there are economies of scale.

It is rather hard to break even on a fund of $10 million to $20 million, but at $1 billion in assets, it is possible to charge fees less than 0.5% of assets for a total of $5 million in management expenses. Now it is time to ask: how much is a fair price for all this? Consider the amount of money the funds in Table 12.2 charged in 2001, along with the amount of money they lost for their investors. The Vanguard S&P 500 Fund is included at the bottom for reference.

Next, transaction costs for buying and selling stocks must be considered. They are not normally considered as part of the management fees and are subtracted before results are posted. Thus, they are somewhat hidden from view and investors should be wary of this. Although every fund must buy stocks for new investors, they don't have to churn their portfolio (but many do).

Extensive marketing fees, or often charged as what are known as 12-b1 fees, are particularly objectionable. They perform absolutely no useful function for investors whether they in are active or indexed funds. Fund groups like them because they bring in new clients, and new clients mean bigger fee payouts. In my view, funds with 12-b1 fees that exceed 0.05% of assets should be eliminated from consideration as a matter of course.

Many active funds have sales commissions or "loads" to pay brokers and middlemen. According to former star fund manager Peter Lynch, "If you plan to stick with a fund for several years, 2–5 percent you paid to get into it will prove insignificant."[1] That's not what the numbers say. Consider what 5% paid to Magellan itself or a broker instead of being reinvested does to a portfolio using Magellan's own annualized rate of return in the past 10 years.

Be aware that many funds pay out commissions over time from their own management fees. A fund with a high management fee sold through a broker with no load is often such an animal. Most commissions are paid up front via "front loads." To calculate their effect, one simply reduces the initial investment by the fee amount for comparison purposes. This strategy is the most straightforward way for a fund to pay a broker for

TABLE 12.2   ACTIVE VERSUS PASSIVE FUNDS

FUND NAME	ANNUAL FEES AS % OF ASSET	ANNUAL RETURN 2001
Janus	0.83%	−26.10
Janus 2	1.00%	−25.50
Janus Adviser Aggressive Gr	0.67%	−39.02
Janus Adviser Balanced	1.17%	−4.92
Janus Adviser Capital Appr	0.67%	−21.83
Janus Adviser Equity Inc	1.75%	−13.03
Janus Adviser Growth	1.17%	−23.23
Janus Adviser Growth & Inc	1.52%	−12.82
Janus Adviser Strategic Val	1.75%	−14.66
Janus Balanced	0.83%	−5.04
Janus Core Equity	0.93%	−12.11
Janus Enterprise	0.90%	−39.93
Janus Global Life Sciences	0.91%	−18.09
Janus Global Technology	0.90%	−39.96
Janus Growth & Income	0.86%	−14.37
Janus Mercury	0.88%	−29.78
Janus Olympus	0.89%	−32.05
Janus Orion	1.12%	−14.69
Janus Special Situations	0.94%	−16.00
Janus Strategic Value	0.91%	−11.74
Janus Twenty	0.84%	−29.20
Janus Venture	0.86%	−11.93
Vanguard 500 Index	**0.18%**	**−12.02**

SOURCE: Morningstar

representing a mutual fund, but it strikes most investors as not exactly the kind of relationship they thought they had with their broker. Isn't the broker supposed to represent the client?

Back-load funds take their sales fees upon redemption. This type of load makes more sense as a disciplining tool. Investors who charge in and out of funds create havoc. They force fund managers to keep large reserves of cash on hand instead of being fully invested and generate capital gains distributions for the hapless investors who decide to remain.

TABLE 12.3   EXPENSIVE INDEX FUNDS

INDEX FUND	TICKER	TOTAL EXPENSE RATIO	INDEX TRACKED
Morgan Stanley S&P 500 Index B	SPIBX	1.50%	S&P 500
MainStay Equity Index A	MCSEX	0.92%	S&P 500
AXP Small Company Index A	ISIAX	0.90%	S&P SmallCap 600

SOURCE: Morningstar data as of 4/30/2002

These loads continue to be hefty. According to Financial Research Corp. of Boston, up from 4.86% in 1997, the average load in 2002 is an astounding 5.2%.[2]

Most unpardonable are index funds that charge high annual fees or sales commissions (loads). These are mostly offered by supermarket fund groups that emphasize active funds with high fees but don't want to lose any clients. "You want an index fund? We can do that!" Consider the gall of the firms in Table 12.3 for charging these hefty fees for what is essentially a commodity.

ON FINANCIAL ADVISORS

Financial advisors and brokers who act as advisors by charging a "wrap" or asset-based fee increasingly are supporting index funds as a professional class. As relatively dispassionate observers (normally they are paid only by the investor), they gain nothing when the crush of high-fee funds catches up with the investor. In fact, they have much to lose; their annual income stream comes from advising the client. Index funds leave more room for the advisor fee. There is only so much cash that can be taken out of clients' account without having them notice, and index funds relieve the pressure all around. It is one thing to ask an investor to pay a 5% load and 2% per year for a star fund, but to add on another 0.5% or 1% for a financial advisor? Investors won't pay it, so the advisor becomes the natural advocate of indexing.

Clearly, some level of professional advice is desirable for many investors and perhaps even required for certain ones who need extra hand-holding. The typical financial advisor who is paid by the client and not by a mutual fund or brokerage firm is compensated without clear conflict of interest. Financial advisors are welcome medicine to the confused investor who needs a little handholding and personal guidance. Like any medicine, they should be used appropriately.

The main issue with full-service financial advisors is that for portfolios of less than $250,000, it doesn't make sense. It is too expensive for the investor, and the advisors can barely cover their costs. Many observers feel the minimum portfolio size is twice that. Modest advisory fees will keep an investor on track with a sensible asset allocation strategy, while excessive advisory fees will cause drag for a portfolio just like any other fees. The index investor is encouraged to view these fees with the same scrutiny as the fees of active funds. Certainly, the laws of mathematics are no different for one than for the other. A fee paid to a financial advisor is lost just as surely as a fee extracted by a mutual fund. Well, not entirely lost. In our view advisors literally earn back some of their fees from occasional rebalancing alone. This is the practice of selling asset classes when they are high to buy others when they are low 137sell high, it's the point of investing, isn't it? The only problem is that few index investors do it on their own.

"The biggest problem in the investment area is procrastination. People want to do it but don't get around to it," said Rick Ferri of Portfolio Solutions, a vigorous advocate of efficient index investing. He estimates that rebalancing alone can gain an investor 0.2% or more on average per year. We think that may understate this important discipline.

In our view, a 0.25% management fee is an absolute bargain, 0.5% is fair, and anything over that needs to be justified by additional service. As with fund expenses, the higher the advisor fee, the more that advice had better be extra good. There is a fair degree of catch-up to do when an advisor takes 0.5% of assets per year, and at 1%, well, ouch! Consider Figure 12.4.

Does this mean everyone should go their own way, armed with this book and a subscription to *The Wall Street Journal*? Not at all. There is no other financial professional more useful to the investor than a financial advisor, save the CPA. So why not pay them like you would the CPA, by the hour or by the project? Paying by percentage of asset value is fine if it works out to a reasonable fee. Like the CPA, the advisor has certain overhead expenses, but they are not huge. Larger portfolios are surely going to be more complicated to handle than smaller ones, but discounts should apply for volume.

Financial advisors have their expenses, too. It is still very much a cottage industry. The high personal contact required by customers has meant that efforts to gain efficiencies through scale, computers, and telecommunications in advising have been a little slower than in other parts of the financial services. Advisors must still dispense their advice one-on-one and send out their monthly newsletters to clients as they have always done. They must market in person. Rick Ferri estimates that it takes at least $1000 in revenue to break even on a client with basic service, and that assumes an outfit with low overhead. Like any happy arrangement, it has to work for both parties.

In most cases, advisors have a stock set of portfolios, say 10 or 20, designed for various types of persons. If two investors approach them with the same risk profile, time horizon, and financial goals, but one has

FIGURE 12.4   ADVISOR FEE DRAG AS PERCENTAGE OF FUND OVER TIME

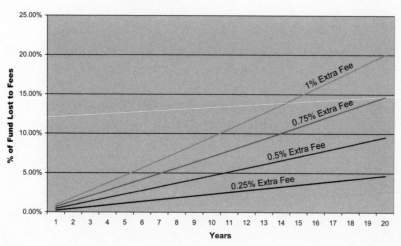

$500,000 and the other has $1,000,000, do you think the second will receive twice as much service? This investor will receive more on average to be sure due to inevitable additional complexity, but not likely twice as much. Advisors quite rightly put many of their clients in a modest number of portfolio models and products they know well, modified to suit investor circumstances. My advice is to keep fees aligned with actual services rendered. There is a long practice of shopping around for competitive fees in institutional investing, and volume discounts are the rule, not the exception. There is no reason retail investors cannot adopt this philosophy. Most advisors specializing in indexing offer flexible payment schedules, including volume discounts, set annual fees, and project and hourly rates. If you don't have $250,000 to invest, well, keep reading books like this and visiting sites like IndexFunds.com, because it doesn't make sense otherwise.

CHAPTER 13

Avoiding Taxing Activity

Y ou can't evade taxes without going to jail, and you can't avoid taxes without a clever sheltering strategy, but you can help to delay taxes with index funds. Tax-sheltered accounts, from IRAs to 401-k to pension plans, all make the issue irrelevant for many assets. But for those assets that are not covered by such plans, and inevitably every investor has a substantial amount of such vulnerable assets, careful attention should be paid.

After a series of tax reforms in the last two decades, capital gains in the United States have become taxed at a much lower rate than ordinary income for most people. Price appreciation of a stock is a capital gain, while dividends or bond interest is classed as ordinary income. So all else being equal, you want to own stocks that pay few dividends and plow their earnings back into the company to grow the stock price. Bonds are to be avoided. Of course, all else is not equal because bonds offer security that stocks never can. The important fact remains that capital gains are more desirable. They are so desirable that a plausible argument can be made that the run-up in stock valuations (such as high P/E or price/book value ratios) is entirely reasonable given the after-tax superiority of stocks.

Delaying capital gains is the next great precept of tax minimization, and here is where indexing comes in. Equity index funds are extremely tax-efficient because they allow the taxpayer to delay realization of the vast majority of capital gains until it is time to leave the fund. The opposite is true for active funds with a tendency for high turnover (heavy trading), which forces regular payments to Uncle Sam for realization of capital gains.

> Tax Rule: Capital gains are "realized" and taxes on them due when an asset is sold.

The mutual fund is a pooled investment entity in which each investor owns a set portion of the pool of assets, so when taxable gains occur, investors are notified along with the IRS of their portion. Realized gains are declared periodically by funds in what is known as *capital gains distributions*.

The effect of paying taxes early is not nearly as disastrous as the effect of paying unnecessary fees. At least with taxes, everybody must pay—it's just a matter of when. The difference is in the opportunity cost of not being able to earn gains on the tax money paid early on. In Figure 13.1, we compare $10,000 funds with low and high turnover. Given the assumptions in Figure 13.1, including equal returns and fees, we can calculate what will happen purely as an effect of taxation.

As with any asset that compounds with time, the length of the investment period in question is the biggest factor in determining the damage, on both a percentage and absolute basis. Thus, if your time horizon is quite short, then maybe it's not a concern. But most retirement funds are by definition quite long in their time horizon. If you are saving for your children and perhaps for their children, it's hard to say just how long the time horizon is, but it's certainly measured in many decades.

Now for the really cruel trick occasionally played on the earnest active fund investor. In times of market decline, they sometimes pay far more

FIGURE 13.1   TAX EFFECT ON NET ACCUMULATION OF TAXES
OVER TIME

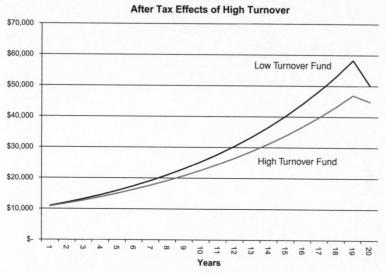

After Tax Effects of High Turnover

Assuming identical 10% fund performance for both funds, common 25% capital gains rate, high turnover fund realizing 50% of its gains per year.
Low turnover fund has no realized gains until Year 20, when fund is sold and all assets taxes paid.

than their fair share of taxes! This happens because, as described above, all taxable gains are pooled during the year and then officially distributed at various points during the year, typically quarterly and at least once near the end of the year. The key to remember is that there is a day of record when the investor is officially liable for the latest period of distributions. Investors who decide to redeem their shares and flee a fund before that date get the full proportional value of capital gains and income but do not get stuck with the tax bill for that quarter. It's the remaining loyal supporters who pay their share!

This is not such a problem when investors come and go in a smooth flow at regular intervals. Of course, that is not what happens in real markets. Money floods into the market in good times, while eager investors chase high historical returns and play the momentum game. When the business cycle turns down, and inevitably it does, investors pull some of their money out of equity funds and seek the shelter of bonds. In true bear markets this happens with a vengeance. (Even though a given year saw a dip in the portfolio's net asset value, inevitably it will hold some items that have unrealized capital gains from previous years' activity.) So the loyal active investor is hit with a double whammy: a terrible year for returns, and unusually high capital gains distributions!

Well, that should be enough for someone new to indexing to consider at the moment. In the next part of this book, we turn to concrete plans of action.

PART II

Taking Action

CHAPTER 14

Financial Planning à La Carte

The best thing that an investment advisor can do for you is to assess your financial needs and design a tailored program to meet them.

—William A. Sherden, *The Fortune Sellers*

Not surprisingly, this book recommends spending a far greater percentage of one's time and money in the critical planning, asset allocation, index selection, and product selection phases than most investment professionals. Since there is no wasted effort from endless absorption of market trivia, fruitless stock picking, or selection of star fund managers, plenty of time is freed up for proper financial planning and for picking assets, indexes, and products.

As a practical matter, filtering out the financial media noise will free up the most time. Investors spend hours every week filling their heads with useless trivia. If anything, it can lead one to costly or risky trading. Following overall economic activity is still useful. With the free time, I recommend investors spend it with their family, friends, and community. They certainly will be happier for it, and I predict they won't be any less wealthy.

Planning is absolutely critical but underappreciated by most Wall Street professionals. This is no surprise, as they do not benefit from planning. It is a relatively unprofitable business because it is required infrequently, can be done by small firms such as CPA practices or small financial advisor offices, is viewed by investors as a commodity, and offers no steady annual income. Investors will be better off if they turn the normal approach on its head. Financial planning and objective advice are not commodities, but rather a highly differentiated product. Stock picking is not a highly differentiated product but rather a commodity (and one worth very little if anything). The cost of performing planning should be considered. A simple graph of how much to spend based on one's portfolio offers a rule of thumb for how deep a financial plan should be. Some example portfolios show typical suggestions for various types of investors.

At some point it is necessary to put discussions of the merits of indexing and various asset class weightings aside and actually invest. On the one hand, the indexer is keenly aware of the importance of placing investments in the right asset allocations and the right funds so as to avoid costly trading. On the other hand, any delay in investing somewhere creates cash drag. Simply parking one's cash in money market funds will barely cover inflation.

Making a wrong early asset allocation is less of a concern to active traders because they will likely have turned over their entire portfolio within a year. However, the indexer struggles over this. Many active investors are taught to construct a good financial plan once, perform crude asset allocation, and really focus on finding a great star mutual fund manager. Oh, yes, when that manager fails, they spend a lot more time finding another star manager.

Indexing reverses this recommendation. Develop a good financial plan once, and again every five or ten years or at major milestones. Then, do a really thorough job of asset allocation. Finally, take a modest amount of time selecting fund brands, and be sure to rebalance occasionally. Perhaps the most ignored aspect of indexing among those who enthusiastically call themselves indexers is rebalancing. In particular, reassessment of risk versus reward upon major market run-ups is where I allocate any extra energy.

Since there are many excellent financial planning books out there, this subject is treated briefly here with a view to the indexer. Indexing makes financial planning so easy and thorough because:

1. Time previously spent picking stocks or funds is now freed up.

2. Assets are explicitly delineated, so nonfinancial assets can be easily meshed into a comprehensive plan.

A comprehensive plan is not as easy to do when your portfolio drifts from one style to another as managers change their minds and as you switch between funds.

A standard checklist of goals to develop includes:

1. Retirement income

2. Medical care for life

3. Comfortable housing

4. University education for children

5. Travel or hobbies

For each goal, a time period must be attached, along with a degree of importance. Having excellent medical care and comfortable housing for life should rate very highly, along with a modest retirement income at normal retirement ages. Assistance for children's education would come next for most persons, followed by travel and hobbies.

A typical list of resources and tools to achieve these goals might include:

1. Tax-sheltered retirement fund

2. Taxable retirement fund

3. Home equity

4. Income stream

5. Life insurance

6. Medical insurance

At this point planning is often a matter of trying to match the right resource and tool to the right goal.

The key to thorough financial planning is comprehensiveness. What are all the goals you have, what are all the resources you have at your disposal, and what are all the tools that you can use? Do not carve out your investment fund from the rest of your financial life, but rather include it in an overall plan.

For instance, homeowners often have a very valuable real estate asset that may not be included in their overall net worth. Calculating when the mortgage will be paid off is essential, and reserving sufficient cash to do so with a margin of error is equally important. If living in a comfortable home for the rest of one's life is a goal, it needs to be stated explicitly and steps to achieve the goal should be described in detail. At the same time, a house is part of the residential real estate asset class. If its value exceeds the amount owed to the mortgage bank, the owner is said to have equity in it and this equity should explicitly be listed as part of an individual's portfolio.

Likewise, an individual's job should be considered a component of his or her long-term investment portfolio. If individuals have built up a solid career, they control a fairly reliable stream of income. They are subject to various particular risks, such as their own performance and the performance of their company, but they also are subject to industry risk. Most job losses today occur because of industry-wide downturns. In my view, the worker-investor should include this industry risk in the wider portfolio of assets they control.

Many individuals like to invest in their company and their industry because they feel pride and loyalty, which are not terribly sound reasons. Still others invest because they have insight and experience in the company and industry and believe it to be a sound investment. First, I question whether it is easy to make the distinction, but more importantly, where does that leave investors? It leaves them with an even less diversified portfolio, if understood in the larger sense. When Enron went bankrupt, not only did many employees lose their jobs, but they also lost large portions of their retirement portfolios because their 401-k plans were so loaded up with the company stock.

One IndexFunds.com visitor who had accumulated SBC Communications stock in his retirement account over a number of years working for the regional telephone giant posted a message on our bulletin board asking how he might diversify away his exposure to the company. He offered his portfolio, a fairly typical smattering of U.S. stock funds, including an S&P 500 fund. I decided to look up SBC's chart next to see what it looked like next to the S&P in recent years (see Figure 14.1).

SBC outperformed the S&P 500, and it also tended to move predictably with it in the same directions. What was the actual risk presented by his SBC ownership, and what was the solution? In my view, his SBC holdings were sufficiently correlated with the S&P 500 that he had a hidden overweighting there. SBC's outsized performance would surely slow down in the not too distant future (I am a reversion to the mean devotee to the last), but I suspected that its underlying tendency to mirror the direction of the S&P would remain. He viewed it as a modest concentration in an S&P 500 fund in his SBC holdings, pointing out that SBC's correlation coefficient with the S&P 500 was below 80%. He was reading

FIGURE 14.1   CHART OF SBC NEXT TO S&P 500—DOES SBC FOLLOW THE S&P 500?

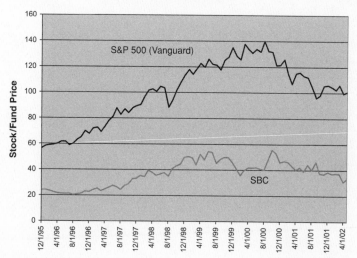

off the number, and I was looking at the chart. My suggestion was to consider lowering the explicit S&P 500 exposure in his portfolio. He disagreed. Vive la difference!

Hiring a financial planner is a fine idea, especially to do an initial portfolio review. As mentioned, it is preferable if the person is truly a planner first and foremost, and not just doing it as a way to gather brokerage or insurance business. However, if you have already selected an advisor or broker, and he or she happens to do planning as well, there is no harm in that. At this point it becomes a matter of asset allocation, and asset class picks should always be reviewed to see if they agree with the investor's original plan.

CHAPTER 15

Know Your Indexes

In finance, indexes are representations of economic activity or assets. Normally, this means a basket of stocks, but it can also include bonds, real estate, commodities, and even noninvestment economic activity. While this book is focused on U.S. activity, nearly every country that trades company stock has a country index that represents its leading companies. Larger industrial countries may have dozens of well-known indexes.

Although financial indexes are the main concern of this book, taking note of the many other types of indexes keeps us aware of how just about everything today is tracked. The Consumer's Price Index (CPI), for instance, is the U.S. Bureau of Labor Statistics measure of prices paid for a market basket of consumer goods and services by an urban American family. In many contracts calling for inflation protection, it is the figure used as a stand-in for inflation. Economists use the CPI to see how quickly the economy is heating up, while labor unions use it to gauge how much purchasing power their members' salaries are bringing them.

Various consumer confidence indexes came into the spotlight after the terrorist attacks of September 11. The Michigan Index of Consumer Sentiment interviews about 500 individuals concerning their financial situations and future spending plans. The Conference Board surveys about 5000 households on similar attitudes and also adds questions about employment.

A variety of other government indexes and indicators follow inventory levels, purchasing plans by major corporations, housing starts, capital expenditure decisions, etc. One note of caution about economic activity indexes. They are helpful at times for sensing general trends but are often inaccurate. The methodology involves subjective opinion and perhaps the plans of purchasing managers who can change their minds later. It cannot be compared to the firm stance of an equity index. The equity index reflects a series of actual commitments of capital in buy or sell decisions that cannot be undone.

If you follow economic benchmarks, you will note that many have multiple revisions for several months following the original announcement! Data is sifted through again and revised, often with major differences over time. Their accuracy leaves much to be desired, causing many investors to act on poor data. Finally, the relation of the economic indicators to anything meaningful to investors can be tenuous. The relationship of consumer confidence to consumer spending, which presumably would tip off favorable times for companies in cyclical consumer goods and services, for instance, is minimal according to accountants at Deloitte Research, who tried in vain to find a clear statistical tie over the last two decades of the twentieth century with a research paper in 2002 entitled "Why You Should Have No Confidence in Consumer Confidence."[1] This is why, as we examined previously, it is very hard for fund managers to gain an edge over their competitors. There are lots of economic indicators moving in every direction, but what should we make of them all at any given point in time?

HOW INDEXES ARE CONSTRUCTED

Normally, indexes are market capitalization-weighted, or "cap-weighted" in common usage. This just means the larger companies make up a bigger part of the list than the smaller ones, in proportion to their value or market capitalization, as implied by their stock price. General Electric, for instance, can make up 4% or more of the S&P 500 when its total market worth is $370 billion, whereas one of the smaller companies may occupy only a tiny fraction of the index. If GE goes up sharply relative to the other components, this index will climb far faster than if a small company spikes. Mobil Oil, Microsoft, and Ford Motor Company are a big part of the U.S. economy, and to invest in the U.S. economy you must weight these giants more heavily than other firms (see Table 15.1). The reason for weighting by market capitalization is to make the index more representative of the actual economic activity and value in the asset class.

A price-weighted index overweights the companies with higher listed stock prices. Richard Ciuba, account development executive in the Indexing Group at Dow Jones, explains why the Dow Jones Industrial Average

TABLE 15.1   HOW A TYPICAL INDEX WEIGHTS ITS COMPONENTS

	PRICE	NO. OF SHARES OUTSTANDING	MARKET CAPITALIZATION
Stock A	$50.00	1600	$80,000.00
Stock B	$100.00	200	$20,000.00
Total	$150.00	1800	$100,000.00
	INDEX WEIGHTING	PORTFOLIO AMOUNTS	NO. OF SHARES
Value-Weighted Index			
Stock A	0.8	$800.00	16
Stock B	0.2	$200.00	2
Price-Weighted Index			
Stock A	0.33	$333.33	6.67
Stock B	0.67	$666.67	6.67
Equally-Weighted Index			
Stock A	0.50	$500.00	10
Stock B	0.50	$500.00	5

(DJIA) is price-weighted: "The index was created 100 years ago at a time when the main emphasis was on fixed-income instruments. It was simply computed as the average price of the 12 stocks that made up the index. The creators did not anticipate stock splits, run-offs, takeovers, mergers and acquisitions."[2]

Early in this century, high prices were synonymous with larger companies and higher market caps, so price weighting approximated market-cap weighting. Things have obviously changed, but the old method is still used for computing the index. Why is the DJIA at 10,000 if it is supposed to be the average price of the 30 stocks in the index today? It is because it has been adjusted every time a stock split, a company paid a dividend of more than 10%, or a company in the group was replaced by another. The Japanese Nikkei 225 is also price-weighted. I do not recommend using these indexes.

An equally-weighted index makes no distinction between large and small companies, both of which are given equal weighting. Since there are many more small companies than large ones, this strategy greatly emphasizes small companies relative to their economic activity. Table 15.2 is an index of two stocks constructed with each method shows how overweighting of high-priced stocks occurs in price-weighting and how overweighting of small-cap stocks occurs in the equally-weighted index.

Nearly every index created today is market-weighted. This method best manages to capture the underlying economic activity the investor wants to participate in. Traditional market capitalization-based means the indexes buy stocks in relation to their total value as calculated by the stock price multiplied by all stock outstanding. Float-based indexes are a version that ignores all stock held privately, typically by company founders. With traditional capitalization-weighted indexes, the argument can be made that the investor is investing in the broader economy, participating even in those shares not held by the public, and therefore quite broadly diversified. But most experts agree that float-based indexes are clearly superior. The argument here is that the investor is investing in the largest portion of the economy where stocks are actively and fairly traded. Liquidity has a higher premium here. The data clearly appears to favor float-based indexes modestly over time. Salomon Smith Barney, which has conducted float-based U.S. and global indexes, has consistently beaten those of rival Morgan Stanley. Morgan Stanley finally relented in the late

TABLE 15.2   SIMPLE INDEX USING EACH METHOD

	PRICE	NO. OF SHARES OUTSTANDING	MARKET CAPITALIZATION
Stock A	$40.00	1600	$64,000.00
Stock B	$120.00	200	$24,000.00
Total	$160.00	1800	$88,000.00
	NEW INDEX WEIGHTING	NEW PORTFOLIO AMOUNTS	NEW PORTFOLIO WEIGHTS
Value-Weighted Index: New Index Value = 88			
Stock A	0.73	$640.00	0.73
Stock B	0.27	$240.00	0.27
Total		$880.00	
Price-Weighted Index: New Index Value = 106.67			
Stock A	0.25	$266.67	0.25
Stock B	0.75	$800.00	0.75
Total		$1,066.67	
Equally-Weighted Index: New Index Value = 100			
Stock A	0.50	$400.00	0.4
Stock B	0.50	$600.00	0.6
Total		$1,000.00	

1990s and conducted a multi-year transition to float-based indexes. The U.S. powerhouse, S&P, is well aware of the issue, and I expect all of its U.S. indexes to gravitate towards float basis over time.

HISTORY

Wells Fargo Bank's institutional investment branch is generally credited with creating the first index fund. In 1969 bank managers William Fouse and John McQuown used the latest academic research to land an account holding $6 million for the Samsonite Corporation. An equal amount of dollars was allocated to each of the equities listed on the New York Stock Exchange. There were 1500 stocks trading on the NYSE at the time. Requirements to frequently maintain the weighting with gyrating stock prices created huge transaction costs. The equal-weighting strategy, which ensured perfect diversification by company, was replaced with capitalization weighting, which provides a more representative view of the economy and therefore better economic diversification. It remains the dominant method and seems to satisfy most investors.

A number of experiments in institutional investing occurred until John Bogle at the Vanguard Group in 1975 decided to create the S&P 500 Index Fund for retail investors. It is now running neck and neck with Fidelity Magellan for the title of the largest equity fund in the world.

Indexes, it should be reaffirmed, need not be public to be legitimate. Anyone can create an index. As long as the components of a basket of stocks make sense together and can be followed easily, we view it as an index. Ultimately, an index is just a reasonable representation of an attractive asset class. If you assemble all the stocks that sell 80% or more of their products to teenagers, you have a legitimate index. If you can put on a list all the Asian banks with at least 50% of revenues coming from business outside their primary market, you also have an index. Never mind that these teenager or multinational Asian banking indexes are found nowhere in the media. If they can be tracked reliably and represent a group of attractive assets for your portfolio, they may be useful.

Custom indexes are less fanciful than it might seem, because institutional investors have been pursuing them for years in hopes of creating a total portfolio that minimizes transaction costs and decreases volatility (risk). Typically, they are a slight variant of a well-known index that does not rebalance quite so quickly as the index rules require or that samples in a less precise manner to keep trades down. For individual investors custom indexes may be purchased in the so-called folio or portfolio concept, available in many brokerages and from specialty firms such as ShareBuilder and FOLIOfn. It's an intriguing concept that is part fund and part brokerage purchase. You can create your own custom index or folio from a wide variety of funds, and purchase or sell them as a block for a fraction of what it would have cost to buy the individual stocks. Many financial advisors suggest that investors stay away from long-term bonds, because they tend to correlate with bear markets in equities. If protection from down equity markets is what the investor wants, they should grab short-term bonds, whose interest rates may rise and fall more quickly but whose principal value will be far more stable.

In selecting indexes to best represent an asset class, there are a few principles to keep in mind. Institutional and high-net worth investors may want to spend the extra time worrying about which is the perfect index in a particular asset class, and they have a lot more money to hire experts to look into all the different interactions. But most investors should not care about the finer points of index weighting. Who cares if one owns 3.5% or 4% of Microsoft stock in a large-cap index? Over the long run, is it really that important, because most of a portfolio's return is based on asset allocation and not on individual stocks?

Some indexes within the same asset class may emphasize value stocks a bit more, others emphasize old-economy stocks, and still others are weighted on stocks actually traded on the open market as opposed to owned privately. The key is not to trade unnecessarily.

SLICING AND DICING

Slicing and dicing, or the practice of dividing the market into multiple indexes, is practiced successfully and thoughtfully by many advanced indexers and advisors. Its current main use is to overweight value over growth. However, slicing can be elegant or sloppy. One basic principle of index selection is to never divide an asset class into adjacent sectors if you intend to treat the class as a whole, because stocks can drift between sectors, which leads to transaction costs.

For instance, if you really want to own and hold the total stock market for the long term, don't buy the S&P 500 along with the Wilshire 4500, its extended market complement (the two together in the right proportions are equivalent to the Wilshire 5000, which is often regarded as a pretty good approximation of the total U.S. stock market). Just buy the Wilshire 5000 and be done with it.

Why? There is a steady hidden cost to slicing. Indexes have rules about which stocks may fit in them, and over time stocks will tend to drift in and out of indexes. As they do, the investor's fund is obliged to buy or sell them and pay for transaction costs. Estimates vary, but visible and hidden transaction costs can amount to 1% or more of the value of the stocks in question. It depends how many stocks leave or join the index each year, but the final cost is likely to be less than 0.10% of the entire fund and usually less. But with adjacent indexes the very same stocks that leave one index will immediately join another. The investor is actually selling and then buying back exactly the same stock!

An example came up with a visitor to IndexFunds.com, whose portfolio is shown in Table 15.3. This investor seemed intent on permanently overweighting small-cap value. There probably was no need to buy small-cap value and growth separately. Unless there were other constraints, the portfolio in Table 15.4 would have achieved the same long-term objectives.

TABLE 15.3   EXAMPLE VISITOR PORTFOLIO WITH INEFFICIENT ADJACENT INDEXES

INDEX	PERCENTAGE
S&P 500	2%
Total Market	4%
Extended Market	4%
Large Value	4%
Small Value	6%
Health Care Fund	5%
European	3.50%
Pacific	3.50%
International Value Fund	4%
Emerging Mkts.	5%
REIT	6%
Gold & Precious Metals	4%
Short-Term Bond	24.50%
Short-Term Corporate Bond Fund	24.50%

TABLE 15.4   MORE EFFICIENT VERSION OF VISITOR PORT-
FOLIO (ASSUMES **S&P 500** IS **75%** AND EXTENDED
MARKET IS REMAINING **25%** OF TOTAL MARKET)

INDEX	OLD PERCENTAGE	MORE EFFICIENT EQUIVALENT
S&P 500	2%	0
Total Market	4%	6.67%
Extended Market	4%	3.33%
Large Value	4%	4%
Small Value	6%	6%
Health Care Fund	5%	5%
European	3.50%	3.50%
Pacific	3.50%	3.50%
International Value Fund	4%	4%
Emerging Mkts.	5%	5%
REIT	6%	6%
Gold & Precious Metals	4%	4%
Short-Term Bond	24.50%	24.50%
Short-Term Corp. Bond Fund	24.50%	24.50%

POPULARITY OF AN INDEX

The popularity of an index is a double-edged sword. It does make it easier if one's portfolio is based on a popular index widely disseminated in
the media, but it also means that investors may ignore diversification and
other important issues in favor of ease of tracking. International indexes
are an excellent example of this. For investors of any nationality, major
domestic indexes are easy to follow, whereas international ones are less so.
They are not followed so closely in the media and are not topics of common conversation. They seem foreign. Well, indeed, they are foreign. That's
a good thing. They offer diversification away from the investor's own

economy. However, tracking lesser indexes may be a burden and cause unease, so they are not right for everyone.

Financial advisors try to educate investors as best they can, but in the end it is best to stick with what the investor understands. The danger of an investor panicking at the wrong moment and selling an index at a market low in order to follow the herd towards the lofty valuation of a more popular index is too great. As Jim Novakoff, president of financial advisors Novakoff & Co., puts it, "If you are creating a portfolio that tracks to U.S. expectations you will want to underweight international."[3]

This is also true of small-cap U.S. indexes, which tend not to move in lockstep with better publicized large-cap indexes such as the Dow Jones Industrials. Although many believe indexes are created in an entirely mechanical manner, this is not true. The Dow Jones Industrials and many S&P indexes, to name a few, are created by committee vote of internal "editors." This can be a good thing.

Consider the case of small caps, where the most popular index is probably the Russell 2000, an index created in automated fashion once a year without discretion. According to Goldman Sachs, the S&P Smallcap 600 outperformed the Russell 2000 by 47% during the period January 1994 to March 2002! Yet the indexes remained highly correlated at around 0.97 during that period, according to Goldman Sachs. How could two indexes that directionally move in lockstep be so far apart?

The Russell 2000 is rebalanced once a year in a mechanical manner based purely on market capitalization on May 31. Unfortunate timing in 1999 and 2000 had start-up technology companies with huge annual losses, pitiful revenues, and few demonstrably loyal customers showing up as small companies. Remember, U.S. small companies can still be worth hundreds of millions of dollars. Volatility and high turnover were the predictable result.

The S&P index, on the other hand, is overseen by a selection committee that requires four quarters of profitability. This means it is perennially underweighted in technology, which abounds in hot new firms that have not yet turned the profitability corner. The committee from time to time may put one firm ahead of another if its industrial sector is poorly represented in the index, and it can make decisions throughout the year as market events dictate.

Table 15.5 lists the indexes we recommend in each major asset class, along with alternative indexes investors may want to consider. A little background on key indexes may prove useful to understanding their role in a U.S. investment portfolio.

DOW JONES

Dow Jones, publisher of *The Wall Street Journal,* is a media company, not really an index company. They have modern indexes, but the Dow Jones Industrials, probably the most widely followed index in the country, is not one of them. It is unrepresentative of the nation's economy because

TABLE 15.5   RECOMMENDED INDEXES

Barra Large Cap Growth	Russell 1000 Growth
Barra Large Cap Value	Russell 1000 Value
Barra MidCap Growth	Russell 2000
Barra MidCap Value	Russell 2000 Growth
Barra SmallCap Growth	Russell 2000 Value
Barra SmallCap Value	Russell 3000
Dow Jones Industrial	Russell Midcap Growth
Dow Jones Large Growth	Russell Midcap Value
Dow Jones Large Value	Russell Top 200 Growth
Dow Jones Midcap Growth	Russell Top 200 Value
Dow Jones Midcap Value	Standard & Poor's 100
Dow Jones Small Growth	Standard & Poor's 500
Dow Jones Small Value	Standard & Poor's Midcap 400
MSCI EAFE	Standard & Poor's Smallcap 600
NASDAQ Composite	Wilshire 4500
NYSE Composite	Wilshire 5000
Pacific Stock Exchange Tech 100	Wilshire Large Cap 750
Russell 1000	Wilshire Large Growth

it follows very large, generally old-line companies. Technology and service firms are poorly represented. Like S&P, committees decide upon the membership in many of its indexes. It has many popular industrial sector indexes, such as the Dow Jones Transportation Index.

STANDARD & POOR'S

Standard & Poor's is very serious about its role as an index provider, and its unique approach is to add judgment to most of its indexes concerning component member selection. It does not automatically include rising companies in an index, but generally presents their candidacy before a committee responsible for the index. Rules for inclusion stress repeated financial performance, fundamental industrial output (as opposed to a holding company simply owning shares in other firms), and a small dose of subjective judgment.

NASDAQ

Many indexes are based on stock exchanges. The Nasdaq Composite, for instance, is a popular index that follows companies listed on the Nasdaq, the independent and relatively tech-heavy U.S. stock exchange. It's also one of the most volatile. The performance of the QQQ ETF following the 100 largest Nasdaq stocks in the late 1990s and early 2000s resembles the run-up and run-down of the Great Crash of 1929. At one point investors were down over 70%!

RUSSELL

A serious indexing house and private money management firm for institutions, Russell indexes run the gamut of U.S. asset classes. The Russell 2000 is its most famous index. It is often used to represent small U.S. companies. This index contains the 2000 smallest stocks in the Russell 3000, itself an index of the 3000 largest stocks in the United States. The big complaint about the Russell indexes tends to be their turnover. Companies come and go enough to make transaction costs noticeable.

WILSHIRE

Wilshire also is a serious indexing outfit with money management services for institutions. The Wilshire 5000 is one of the broadest benchmarks of U.S. stocks. It's what most professionals mean by *total market* in the United States. It tracks the returns of most publicly traded U.S. stocks. Currently there are roughly 7000 stocks in the index, and many are quite small and trade infrequently with low volumes. Most funds that follow it use a sampling technique.

BARRA

This is another small, serious index shop. Barra operates a little like Russell and Wilshire and maintains a whole slew of U.S. indexes. Their division between growth and value is based on price/book value. Commentators on IndexFunds.com have pointed out that Barra's indexes act differently than Wilshire or Russell ones due to Barra's simplified methodology.

INTERNATIONAL INDEXES

Virtually every country has a major index, and industrialized economies have dozens. Foreign stocks and index funds that contain them are expensive to buy for U.S. investors, and correlations between all markets have risen. But in our view the United States in 2002 is still fully valued and international indexes still offer tremendous opportunity to diversify, especially in emerging markets. The problem is to know where and how to avoid corruption, taxation, and, of course, the ever-present international stock trading costs.

In Europe, traditional indexes from the largest economies include the German DAX, English FTSE 100, and French CAC 40. Euronext, a joint venture of the Paris, Amsterdam, and Brussels bourses (exchanges) is a new favorite. Expect more pan-European indexes.

For Japan, the best-known index is the Nikkei, a traditional price-weighted index similar to the Dow Industrials. Big firms in old-line industries are favored, and it does not represent the new Japanese economy.

Given all the conflicts of interest between these giants, we prefer the Topix, a broader index representing the Tokyo Stock Exchange, the country's largest.

Don't forget the Toronto Stock Exchange 300, bigger in valuation than most people realize. Australia's All Ordinaries, while not in valuation a large index, exhibited during the Asian contagion of the late 1990s a remarkable degree of resilience and stability. Hong Kong's Hang Seng has seen volatility but is the index nerve center of Asia along with the Taiwan Weighted and the Singapore Straights Times Index. Also certain to become an important index is China's Shanghai Composite.

MORGAN STANLEY

The giant of international indexing, its Europe, Australia, and Far East (EAFE) index is the dominant non-U.S. benchmark. It has many others representing nearly every asset class, including those in the United States. Morgan Stanley was severely criticized by the indexing community regarding the EAFE for one thing it could do nothing about and for another that it took too long to correct.

The first was the sheer fact that just about every active fund was able to trounce the well-known EAFE during the late 1980s and 1990s simply by underweighting Japan. Of course, an indexer could have done the same by buying global indexes without Japan. But since most uninformed investors knew as little about international activity as they did about indexing, many believed that active managers were actually "beating the market" in international stocks. To make matters worse, many pension funds were simply offering EAFE-based funds and nothing more to their employees for operational simplicity, and many institutional funds with uncritical investment committees did not question the merit of investing in Japan. "How can you be an indexer if you ignore part of the market?" was their simplistic approach. Anyway, it was a disaster for the average international index investor.

Another problem Morgan Stanley had that it failed to address promptly was its insistence for so many years on market capitalization-weighted indexes, where a component is ranked based on its implied market capitalization, versus float-weighted ones, where a component is based on its actual publicly traded shares only. Once again, in Japan this created mischief, as firms with tiny amounts of publicly available shares and inflated valuations became a large part of the index. Many firms owned (and still do) shares in each other. In essence it was a shell game and EAFE investors got the empty shell when Japanese cross-ownership began to unravel. Worst of all, funds had to make a costly transition at the end of the century as Morgan Stanley announced its inevitable transition. Overall, its indexes fared poorly in comparison to float-based ones. At this point Morgan has only float indexes and appears completely up-to-date.

SALOMON SMITH BARNEY

This is a lesser-known index provider that in our view has had modern float-based indexes for years. Its indexes cover the gamut of world markets, including the United States.

LEHMAN BROTHERS

They maintain an assortment of indexes for bonds and other fixed-income instruments.

FORTUNE

Fortune is the premier maintainer of U.S. corporate lists—the best U.S. companies to work for, the highest revenue, etc. As such it is one of the best sources for building custom indexes because it ranks firms on more than just financial accounting numbers. Its most popular formal indexes include the Fortune 500 Index of large U.S. corporations and the e-50 Index of large technology firms.

CHAPTER 16

Model Portfolios

Examples of typical portfolios, or model portfolios, are often where indexers like to begin. They pick a portfolio that meets their needs and modify it to suit them. In theory, investors should build their portfolios from scratch out of their strategy and acceptance of schools of thought. In practice, investors (and their advisors) inevitably sift through what others have done until they find something that feels right. Admittedly, it's a bit of a beauty contest, and judgments can be a bit subjective. However, it seems to be the way investors actually proceed. There appears to be no way around it. Comfort is an inescapable requirement of the investor, and it might as well be acknowledged.

I actually prefer to call these asset allocations *portfolio models* rather than model portfolios. They are by no means meant to be copied verbatim but rather should be considered and changed in various what-if scenarios until the right one pops up. Considering what most other investors are doing is instructive, but how you decide your exact ratio of bonds versus stocks, domestic versus international, and small versus large caps is a matter of personal choice and individual context. More importantly, it is your money, so think it over! While I try to match portfolios with the types of investors I have seen adopt them, just who should pair up with what portfolio we leave to the reader to decide.

Most indexers eventually make their decisions briefly after examining some "model portfolios." It's like model airplanes or dolls or trains, with one small difference. It's a hobby at first, and things seem quite harmless and playful. Then, all of a sudden, your entire retirement fund is based on some model, so you tend to look at them more carefully.

Investors consider this and that theory and then select the portfolio that looks best. In this light I introduce the following portfolio models, in no particular order.

No. 1: Basic Domestic Stock and Bond Split

It doesn't get simpler than this. This portfolio lets investors focus on basic market risks of equities and making sure they are moderating their risks as they approach retirement. If you don't have a lot of money or time or patience with Wall Street professionals, this is the portfolio for you.

The only big decision is how much you want in stocks versus bonds. The investor can also prepare for retirement (or other milestone) by continually ratcheting down the proportion of stocks and hiking the proportion of bonds. As always, rebalancing should be applied to buy low and sell high, and common sense should allow for an occasional retreat into bonds when stocks are at ridiculous valuations. Thus, what often begins as a 80% to 20% stocks to bonds portfolio for a twenty-something individual (in a reasonably valued market) often moves to 50% to 50% ratio as a person nears retirement. How to divide between stocks and bonds is *the* key financial planning question for which there is no clear answer but many reasonable alternatives. The beauty of this portfolio is that its simplicity focuses the individual on that question to the exclusion of all other distractions.

The portfolio consists of a certain percentage of the total domestic stock market and short- to medium-term bonds. In most major economies the total stock market can generally be purchased in one fund, thereby providing the ultimate in diversification while avoiding index inefficiencies. A good representation of short- to medium-term bonds can also be acquired with a minimum of instruments (see Table 16.1).

Because domestic stock and bond funds (of whatever country the investor is from) are relatively cheap to own, this portfolio is quite efficient in terms of fees. For Europeans, euro-denominated funds with a pan-European portfolio bring instant diversification beyond national boundaries. For Americans and Japanese, many domestic companies derive substantial revenues from abroad and bring to their investors surprising international exposure. For investors of countries with smaller economies, it is probably advisable to seek international exposure.

On the bond side, we recommend bonds maturing in no more than five years and of investment grade. High-yield (junk) bonds should be considered as an alternative to low yields from higher-quality bonds and environments, but only with the understanding that they carry more risk. Likewise, bonds with longer maturities than about five years carry considerable interest rate risk. (If general interest rates rise, the bonds will be committed to subpar income for many years and can fall dramatically in value. The longer the term of the bond, the greater the danger.)

The advantages of indexing over active funds are even greater with bonds than with equity funds. It is even harder to outperform the market

TABLE 16.1   SMALL TABLE OF A TYPICAL STOCK/BOND SPLIT IN A PORTFOLIO

	AGE BRACKETS, ASSUMING INTERMEDIATE RISK PROFILE						
	<25	25–35	35–45	45–55	55–65	65–75	76+
Wilshire 5000 or Russell 3000	80%	70%	60%	50%	40%	30%	20%
Lehman Brothers Short-Term Bond Index or Staggered Short-term Treasuries	20%	30%	40%	50%	60%	70%	80%

in bonds than in stocks. Returns of bonds are low enough already. Don't push them down further with needless management costs.

It is not actually necessary to buy a fund to stay true to a passive, indexing philosophy. Short-term U.S. Treasuries staggered along different time periods can provide essentially no risk and therefore remove the need for diversification. They can also be bought directly at minimal cost by calling the Federal Reserve at 800-722-2678, extension 5.

No. 2: Basic Global Stock and Bond Split

This portfolio is similar to the first one but adds geographical breadth for the investor seeking greater diversification. If the investor is in a smaller or less developed country, then going abroad is a requirement for reasons of diversification and risk control. The entire world's stock markets can be purchased in just a few funds. Although somewhat more expensive because of the extra transaction costs of handling equities across boundaries, this portfolio offers the widest possible diversification. There are even individual funds that come close to delivering the entire investable world economy (see Table 16.2).

Once again, a younger investor may find it advisable to start with 80% or even more in stocks (in a market that is not showing signs of over-valuation) and drop that percentage down over time. Rebalancing is advisable, as always.

TABLE 16.2   INVESTOR PROFILES BY AGE, BASIC GLOBAL
             PORTFOLIO

INVESTOR AGE	YOUNG	MIDDLE-AGE	RETIREMENT
W5000 or R3000	50%	40%	30%
MSCI EAFE	30%	20%	10%
Lehman Short Bond	20%	40%	60%

TABLE 16.3   PORTFOLIO WITH HIGH YIELD

	AGE BRACKETS, ASSUMING INTERMEDIATE RISK PROFILE						
	<25	25–35	35–45	45–55	55–65	65–75	76+
Wilshire 5000 or Russell 3000	80%	70%	60%	50%	40%	30%	20%
Short-Intermediate High Yield	20%	30%	40%	50%	60%	70%	80%

No. 3: Take the High-Yield Road

Where the economy appears reasonably healthy, where overvalued stocks are expected to perform weakly in coming years, and where investment-grade bonds offer anemic yields, opportunistic indexers will often seek out high-yield or "junk" bonds of short- to medium-term duration. This is not meant as a market timing exercise, but rather as a multiyear play if junk appears unequivocally undervalued relative to its alternatives. The logic would be the same for those who recommend value over growth over long periods of time. A fund is indispensable because any one company's bonds could become worthless. They don't call it junk for nothing! Rebalancing can be applied as in any other portfolio. Should junk bonds surge and the investor feels they have become highly valued, it may be prudent to exit entirely. This is expected to be an asset for opportunistic investing (see Table 16.3).

No. 4: Core and Explore

This is our basic recommended approach for the stock portion of the portfolio. It lays a foundation on top of which you may overweight any particular asset class, be it small value, large growth, or a sector. It should not be confused with the similarly named strategies that involve active funds.

The concept is to begin with a certain amount of total market that stays static (core) and overweight other asset classes as one sees fit (explore). There is a version of this philosophy among active fund advisors and

TABLE 16.4   CORE AND EXPLORE

	AGE BRACKETS, ASSUMING INTERMEDIATE RISK PROFILE						
	<25	**25–35**	**35–45**	**45–55**	**55–65**	**65–75**	**76+**
Wilshire 5000 or Russell 3000	40%	35%	30%	25%	20%	15%	10%
Russell 3000 Value	20%	17.5%	15%	12.5%	10%	7.5%	5%
Russell 2000 Value	20%	17.5%	15%	12.5%	10%	7.5%	5%
Lehman Brothers Short-Term Bond Index or Staggered Short-term Treasuries	20%	30%	40%	50%	60%	70%	80%

brokers that recommends indexing large-caps as the core and placing the remainder in active funds to explore. Our version obviously involves indexing throughout.

The explore portion can certainly include the popular international, small-cap, and value classes. Sectors, REITs and other individual plays are also popular and perfectly reasonable. It is assumed as well that part of the portfolio remains in bonds. In Table 16.4 we present a portfolio that over-weights small-cap and value asset classes only because this portfolio has proven so popular in the indexing community.

No. 5: Slice and Dice

This portfolio is very popular among experienced advisors and the more sophisticated investors in our community. Slicing and dicing involves chopping up the market into many asset classes and buying only those that as a group deliver solid returns with modest risk. We hardly endorse this strategy.

In Chapter 15, we noted our reservations that this practice can lead to inefficiencies. As previously mentioned, a questionable use of slicing is when two adjacent indexes such as a small growth and a small value are pur-chased when one comprising them both could have been had. The investor ends up selling stocks frequently from one index just to buy them back into

TABLE 16.5   SLICE AND DICE PORTFOLIO

INVESTOR AGE	YOUNG	MIDDLE-AGE	RETIREMENT
W5000 or R3000	60%	45%	30%
Small Value	20%	15%	10%
Lehman Short Bond	20%	40%	60%

the adjacent index and the result is higher turnover. Of course these problems can be mitigated by melding core and explore with slice and dice. For the serious slicer, such as the many individuals who favor large caps coupled with small value, the portfolio in Table 16.5 makes perfect sense.

No. 6: The Value Seeker

Among indexers value, or stocks with low earnings or cash flow as a percentage of their net assets, is praised widely. Some followers of Eugene Fama and Kenneth French, Richard Haugen, and other theoreticians consider this half of the market as the superior long-term portion. Others view value as an alternative or complementary method to bonds in the quest to moderate risk. In practice many investors simply sleep better at night with value than with growth. In any case, this portfolio jumps right into value full bore without any apologies. It harnesses solid long-term returns with moderate risk and especially greater protection against speculative bubbles (see Table 16.6).

TABLE 16.6   VALUE SEEKER PORTFOLIO

INVESTOR AGE	YOUNG	MIDDLE-AGE	RETIREMENT
S&P 500 or Russell 1000	60%	45%	30%
Russell 2000 Value or S&P SmallCap 600	20%	15%	10%
Lehman Short Bond	20%	40%	60%

No. 7: Growth Quest

The opposite of value is growth, which carries high P/E ratios or price/book value ratios. The beauty of growth is that it harnesses most powerfully the benefits of technological innovation and operational efficiencies. Growth companies are most likely to benefit first from spurts in industrial progress which are expected to continue for the foreseeable future. It seems without question that advances in science and technology are going to continue to accelerate, and the companies that lead that charge will see remarkable increases in revenue and earnings.

The problem, and it is a big problem, is that so many investors have heard the praises of growth that they appear to consistently bid growth stocks up, sometimes to heights that are clearly unreasonable. Many active money managers who are keen to outperform broad benchmarks without regard to risk pursue their recklessness through growth stocks. Completely aside from sophisticated debates on the long-term merits of growth versus value, U.S. growth stocks in recent years have gotten completely out of hand and even after breathtaking drops remained pricey.

For example, the average P/E ratio of the S&P 500 was 31.2 and the price/book ratio was 5.6 in March of 2002. This was well after the Internet and telecom bubbles burst. The bet here is that companies will grow their earnings and book values quickly enough to drop these ratios (based on the original price paid) in half in a handful of years. To us this is a steep hill to climb. See Tables 16.7 and 16.8 for a few growth portfolios.

TABLE 16.7   GROWTH PORTFOLIO

INVESTOR AGE	YOUNG	MIDDLE-AGE	RETIREMENT
S&P 500/Barra Value or Russell 1000 Value	60%	45%	30%
Russell 2000 Value or S&P SmallCap 600 Value	20%	15%	10%
Lehman Short Bond	20%	40%	60%

TABLE 16.8   ALTERNATIVE GROWTH PORTFOLIO

INVESTOR AGE	YOUNG	MIDDLE-AGE	RETIREMENT
S&P 500/Barra Growth or Russell 1000 Growth	60%	45%	30%
Russell 2000 Growth or S&P SmallCap 600 Growth	20%	15%	10%
Lehman Short Bond	20%	40%	60%

NO. 8: BIG IS BEAUTIFUL

There is much to recommend large-company stocks. They are easy to follow, they are relatively cheap to buy and sell (and therefore an index containing them has lower transaction costs), and at least before Enron it also seemed highly unthinkable that a multibillion dollar company could go bankrupt almost overnight.

Over longer periods large-caps do not, however, appear to keep up with small caps. In addition, they have sustained run-ups compared to smaller stocks every decade or two. In the early 1970s the "Nifty Fifty" largest stocks delivered splendid returns relative to small stocks was nearly vaporized, and this happened again to a lesser extent in the late 1990s. In both markets this occurred hand-in-hand with the overvaluation of growth. Large stocks and growth stocks seem to gather momentum during the frothiest markets. This bit of information is by no means helpful for prediction, but the commonsense investor is encouraged to keep it in mind (see Table 16.9).

Clearly, all these portfolio models can be modified and combined as the individual investor sees fit.

TABLE 16.9   LARGE CAP PORTFOLIO

INVESTOR AGE	YOUNG	MIDDLE-AGE	RETIREMENT
S&P 500	80%	50%	20%
Lehman Short Bond	20%	50%	80%

CHAPTER 17

Exchange-Traded Funds

"An ETF is like handing an arsonist a match."

—John Bogle, Founder of the Vanguard Group

"Now that they are giving out the can of gasoline, the question is who at Vanguard is going to light it."

—Augustin Fleites, principal responsible for ETFs, State Street Global Advisors[1]

Exchange-traded funds (ETFs) are a powerful new set of indexing tools every investor should consider using. Exchange-traded funds have a whole slew of advantages and only a few weak spots. Like indexing itself, ETFs are not a fad. In fact, they continue to amaze even their proponents with their growth. Their popularity and growth among all types of investors appears unchecked in up markets and down as they surpass $100 billion and appear headed for $1 trillion in assets in a decade.

An exchange-traded fund is one that, unlike a standard mutual fund, may be traded at any time during the day like a stock. Mutual funds are typically redeemed only at end-of-day prices of the sum of their component stocks, called net asset value (NAV). For an indexer with discipline, reputable ETFs can be a huge boost. They offer:

- Absurdly low annual fees
- Ability to buy and sell at precise price points

- Exceptionally low tax distributions

For the more advanced investor, the ETF also offers:

- Ability to sell short
- Ability to use options (for protection or for speculation)

Although the flexibility of being able to get in and out of a position is what defines the ETF, for the typical buy-and-hold investor its phenomenally low annual management fees are perhaps the most important long-term attraction. Barclays' ETF version of the S&P 500, the iShares S&P 500, for instance, costs a mere 0.08% per year to own in annual expenses. That is less than half the already very fair 0.18% charged by the venerable Vanguard S&P 500 Fund. It's not that Vanguard didn't sharpen its pencils. Notoriously cost-conscious, this firm delivers bare bones fees on all its offerings. It is actually owned by fund investors, so there is no motivation to siphon off cash through high fees.

How does Barclays do it? For one thing, ETF managers are able to loan portions of the portfolio to other institutional investors at a profit, thereby defraying costs. How this happens is beyond the scope of this book, but suffice it to say that it is a regular practice among brokerage firms and is not considered an added risk to the ETF investor.

In addition, the ETF gains cost savings through its unique method of buying and selling stocks for its portfolio. This is not done in the typical manner of a mutual fund, which approaches the stock markets and buys and sells stocks among all traders. Instead, in a somewhat complicated process, special institutional traders called *authorized participants* perform the equivalent by assembling the requisite basket of securities that match the target index for the ETF and presenting them in exchange for newly created ETF shares. The basket of underlying shares is put away for safe-keeping much as gold or other reserves are kept in support of national currencies, which are after all only pieces of paper.

Here it is appropriate to stop and stress that as far as the SEC is concerned, ETFs are as reliable as the underlying stocks they represent. Each financial services firm's application for an ETF is individually scrutinized and approved by the SEC in a lengthy and careful examination of operational checks and balances. This is not your garden variety stock or bond that some company can issue and sell on the open market without intense governmental review. ETFs are much more closely watched.

The basket of stocks that underpins any ETF, in the United States at least, is locked up with the Depository Trust Clearing Corporation, the government-controlled securities clearing agency. Investors sometimes ask why their stock trades take a few days to "settle." The DTCC is the firm that makes sure that stocks go one way and cash goes the other during those few days of settlement. Most investors do not hold actual paper securities but instead let their brokerage firms hold them in "street name," or the name of the brokerage firm, to allow transactions to occur more easily. Thus, if you have confidence that you can sell a stock or bond through brokerage firms and receive your cash, you should have equal confidence that you can sell an ETF with the same result.

ETFs are bought and sold across the open markets, so there are brokerage fees involved. Their significance depends upon the volume, trading costs, and timing involved. A $200,000 position traded through an Internet brokerage firm charging $20 per trade would cost the investor 0.01% of assets, essentially insignificant. On the other hand, a $2,000 position traded through a traditional brokerage firm charging $40 a trade would come to 2%, which is considerable. The investor pays on the way in and on the way out. It can be thought of as a kind of sales load that can vary considerably but offers directly proportional volume discounts. For the long-term buy-and-hold investor, time makes these costs even less significant.

As with any stock that is bought and sold on the open market, there are some hidden transaction costs to keep in mind. One of the most obvious is the bid-ask spread, or difference between the amount the buyer is willing to pay and the seller is willing to take. This gap or spread becomes the incentive for an army of middlemen, called specialists or market makers or other less charitable names, to "cross" bids and asks into actual trades. Otherwise, trades would not get done in a timely manner, or as they say in that part of the industry, the quality and liquidity of trading would decline. With pricing now moving to increments as small as a penny, spreads appear to be steadily shrinking, but they should be accounted for.

A study by Salomon Smith Barney on ETF liquidity found an average bid-ask spread of 0.36%, which declined to 0.13% when weighted for capitalization. This is quite small. Keep in mind that the buyer and seller, in essence, share the cost of the spread, because somewhere in the middle is the theoretical price at which the trade would have been made had the buyer and seller been standing right next to each other. Thus, it is probably fair to apportion about half of the spread to each.

As with all index funds, ETFs do not generally carry impact costs, or the movement of prices away from a major buyer or seller. The baskets are simply spread too thin. Thus, a reasonable transaction cost calculation might include the brokerage fee and half the spread on the way in and the same costs on the way out. Remember that mutual funds also have their own transaction fees. They must buy and sell stocks when cash arrives and leaves. These costs are paid by investors and normally are included in total expense ratios.

After investigating the ETF and traditional mutual fund methods of creating and redeeming shares in ETFs, I concluded (admittedly without an authoritative study) that ETFs have a cleaner transactional process and should be slightly cheaper, before brokerage fees are paid. I don't view ETF total transaction fees of 0.2% as particularly damaging, considering the flexibility it gives you.

Low capital gains tax distributions also are a big benefit for the ETF investor. The comparison IndexFunds.com made between ETFs and mutual funds showed ETFs at a distinct advantage with a few exceptions. In our view, only mutual funds specifically managed for low capital gains distributions could keep up (and this includes many fine mutual funds). This is because of what probably is best described as a loophole. ETFs are created and redeemed not generally by buying and selling stock, but rather by trading in-kind a basket of stocks for a newly created one, the ETF share. It just so happens that the ETF can deliver upon redemption of a share with any cost basis at no penalty to the redeemer. Thus, ETF managers can continually shed low-cost-basis stock and keep high-basis stock. They generally have been able to keep distributions of gains small.

There are certain exceptions. In 2000 Vanguard's S&P 500 fund bested Barclays' S&P 500 ETF. Curiously, the explanation appears to be in the breathtaking growth in assets in Barclays' product, not in fleeing investors. Does this mean that ETF investors don't pay capital gains? Not in the least. They pay, but not much until they sell the actual ETF share, at which point most of the bill becomes due. Since delay is the name of the game, this is the desired result.

Flexibility, the ETF's unique strength, is also its greatest danger to the poorly disciplined investor. "ETFs are brilliantly designed products," admits Vanguard's John Bogle of the Vanguard Group. "They will serve investors well if they buy and hold them for the long-term." Unfortunately, many investors use them in a speculative manner. Bogle cited turnover rates of 3250% for Nasdaq QQQs and 1380% for the S&P SPDRs during most of 2001. "I cannot imagine investors engaging in such speculation can be profiting after trading costs are taken into account," he said.[2]

Here is where the circle is complete. The ironic beauty of the ETF, for the long-term indexer, is that its expenses are being supported in part by institutional hedge funds and twitchy day-traders. Certainly, the latter shouldn't be doing what they are doing, but by-and-hold ETF investors are cheering them on! Hedge funds love ETFs because they can get in and out of a market with lightning speed to make their macroeconomic bets. Will interest rates go up and send the entire market down in a quick correction? If a hedge fund thinks so it can sell its ETF position with one single trade, and buy it back again when prices have settled.

There isn't much evidence that hedge funds and individual day traders trying out this strategy will prosper, and I generally don't recommend it. However, they are welcomed with open arms by the long-term investor because the constant activity surrounding ETFs creates a remarkably liquid market for indexes.

ETFs are a curious and complex creature, and at first they drew criticism for seeming efficiency and liquidity problems. When IndexFunds.com examined each charge, we found most to be unfounded and leveled by individuals with wrong facts and a poor understanding of finance.

Some observers new to ETFs have expressed concern that stated trading volumes for major ETFs are too low and that this should signal much higher spreads. What they misunderstand is that the majority of the liquidity of an ETF occurs among the authorized participants who create and redeem ETFs constantly. Unlike a closed-end fund, where there is no way to quickly redeem shares and where the cost of the fund can stray far from its underlying net asset value, with most ETFs this simply does not happen.

In the United States ETFs are created in three different structures: the *unit investment trust, the management investment company*, and the *grantor trust*. The unit investment trust is used only by a handful of ETFs, but they are some of the largest:

- SPDRs tracking the S&P 500 and other S&P indexes

- Diamond Trust (DIA) tracking the Dow Jones Industrials

- Nasdaq-100 Trust (QQQ) tracking the Nasdaq 100

While perfectly adequate, they are a bit crude in operation. They are restricted from reinvesting dividends, lending securities (to obtain additional revenue), and using derivatives to better track their targets. None of these limitations should concern the beginning investor, but some advanced indexers with large portfolios may want to investigate alternative ETFs using the more common and flexible management investment company structure.

The management investment company is legally much like a mutual fund that trades. Its ability to reinvest dividends is a convenience for most investors. It provides fund managers with a variety of tools to track indexes in the most efficient manner possible. They need not buy every stock of an index, but can instead buy a representative sample and hedge the rest with index derivatives (don't worry, this is the conservative side of the options world, not the speculative). Most ETFs following small-cap and mid-cap stocks use this structure. Barclays' iShares generally use it.

Quite separate from the above two is the grantor trust. More primitive still, it is nonetheless elegant in its own way. It's an ETF that provides the most direct link to underlying securities and does not rebalance. Created in batches, the grantor trust represents a snapshot of an index at one point in time. The number of shares of each component company remains static. Thus, there is no buying or selling of shares to keep with an index, so it avoids these costs. The investor can even take possession of the underlying shares for a small fee and handle the stocks individually.

The disadvantage is that the original index will have drifted away from the fund as some companies grow and others recede. Over time, the portfolio will fail to reflect market valuations and true economic activity. In the U.S., Merrill Lynch has the dominant position among grantor trusts with HOLDRs (Holding Company Depositary Receipts), which are focused on sectors. Unfortunately, many were in highly speculative industries such as telecom, business-to-business Internet companies, and biotech, so many investors took a terrible drubbing in the late 1990s. However, they are much more reasonably priced today!

That Merrill Lynch provides investment banking services for some firms that may end up in the HOLDRs index raised a few eyebrows. It is a potential conflict of interest, but, alas, there are many in every investment arena. Another more dramatic charge was that the occasional surprise announcements of new HOLDRs (priced at the closing NAV of the day chosen by Merrill management) allowed arbitrageurs to jump in to exploit the impending announcements. Arbitraging index changes is possible, but it puts a lot of capital at risk for quite modest a spread, and it just so happens that HOLDRs center on some of the most volatile sectors on the planet. There are no easy pickings there.

Curiously, it is State Street that offers the leading ETF tracking the S&P 500, not Vanguard, which has generally been the pioneer of indexing products. As mentioned briefly before, this story has an interesting history. Vanguard resisted ETFs generally because of founder John Bogle's distaste for traded instruments, but others at the firm saw the writing on the wall and pushed for an ETF version as an extension of its standard mutual fund, to be called Vipers. The idea was that both mutual fund and ETF would share the same vast basket of stocks, but that one would be highly liquid and easily traded. The S&P 500 product never reached the market.

S&P sued Vanguard over a licensing dispute when the group tried to launch an ETF based on the S&P 500 and won an injunction. Vanguard retracted its application before the SEC rather than pay extra fees. It has instead pushed its total market Viper fund following the Wilshire 5000.

CHAPTER 18

Fund Picking, Not Stock Picking

"Liberty, according to my metaphysics . . . is a self-determining power in an intellectual agent. It implies thought and choice and power."

—John Adams

Indexers, as the reader is no doubt aware by now, never pick stocks. But they do pick funds and fund groups. There are differences in how products are structured and in the price and services attached to them. Financial services organizations, like people, have a certain personality. Luckily, there are ample choices of inexpensive, solid funds for just about every major asset class from firms that care about indexing.

In the 1960s and 1970s, cost-conscious investors of all stripes scattered their money around to various no-load funds that appealed to them most in each asset category. By the 1980s, investors began to tire of the headaches of dealing with so many different firms. They gravitated towards companies, often called supermarkets, that had a broad set of offerings. For a while it seemed the supermarkets would kill off all the corner stores, that is, the small, focused fund firms. A countervailing force was the rise of the discount brokerage firm, which was happy to consolidate all fund activity into one account and one monthly statement. All this for a small fee, of course. Fund families returned the favor by becoming brokers as well. Internet brokerage firms in the mid-1990s ensured once and for all absolutely rock-bottom trading costs, instant reporting, and the ability to purchase virtually any stock or fund.

With one discount broker it really isn't hard to build a portfolio with funds with no loads, low transaction costs, and low management costs. Many funds skirt the definition of traditional indexing: inexpensive, passive funds that don't track popular indexes, enhanced funds that create leverage or allow contrarian bets, socially conscious index funds, etc. I encourage an open mind in this regard. We ask the questions: Does it represent one or more asset classes useful to the investor, do its managers charge low fees and keep trading to a minimum, and does it distribute taxable gains parsimoniously?

RECOMMENDED FUNDS

The total list of index funds is quite large, but most can be thrown out for sheer excessive fees, and the remainder may be divided into top-tier list of candidates and another list of perfectly acceptable alternative candidates. There is really only a small number of funds and fund groups that grind down their prices for the true do-it-yourselfer with all options available. All else being equal, I recommend this elite group. However, very commonly investors will do business with a stock broker they like and agree to buy an index fund that is higher priced in recognition of extra handholding. Some investors need that extra level of education and service. In addition, some workers may find that their company retirement programs restrict the list of available funds, so my list contains other viable funds that are priced within reason.

The criteria for recommended funds is that they be from serious index-oriented providers, track reputable and useful indexes efficiently, and keep their fees down. I shy away generally from funds that charge front or deferred loads, or 12b-1 fees. The exception here is withdrawals penalties up to a year or two, which we regard as fair and even necessary in less liquid markets such as high-yield bonds and small-cap stocks. In the case of both ETFs and funds only available through advisors (such as the Dimensional Fund Advisors or DFA funds) investors will face additional transaction or holding costs.

I start with U.S. funds, then examine international, bonds, and sectors. In addition, we follow these lists of traditional funds with a short description of the leading alternative passive investing strategies. This includes "folio" brokerage firms that allow consumers to build passive custom indexes of domestic stocks, essentially allowing them to design their own index fund.

For U.S. asset classes, my picks in each major asset class, including:

- Total market
- Large-cap blend
- Large-cap growth
- Large-cap value
- Mid-cap blend
- Mid-cap growth
- Mid-cap value
- Small-cap blend
- Small-cap growth
- Small-cap value

TOTAL MARKET

I believe it is self-evident that portfolios should start with the domestic total market fund for that portion of the portfolio that is intended to mirror, for the long term, the total market on a capitalization-weighted basis. As mentioned previously, I discourage slicing and dicing in which the slices taken are adjacent and up to the whole because component companies will tend to leave one index only to join another. In my view, the indexer without an advisor or broker can do no wrong by starting with one of several outstanding total market funds (see Table 18.1).

TABLE 18.1   TOTAL MARKET PICKS (IN NO PARTICULAR ORDER)

FUND NAME	TICKER	EXPENSE RATIO
Vanguard Total Stock Market	VTSMX	0.20%
iShares Russell 3000*	IWV	0.20%
Vanguard TSM VIPERs*	VTI	0.15%

*exchange-traded funds, which involve brokerage fees; these fees may change!

As usual, Vanguard figures prominently. Do-it-yourself mutual fund investors will find its plain vanilla Wilshire 5000 fund hard to beat. On the ETF side, it's Barclays against Vanguard. Here is it probably more of a contest between indexes than between funds. Investors should probably decide whether they like Russell 3000 more than Wilshire 5000. Wilshire digs deeper into small company stocks, but both are quite broad.

Some Reasonable Alternatives

There are plenty of acceptable funds with higher loads sold through brokers and mutual funds with excellent service. We have mixed feelings about them but note generally that if your advisor diligently rebalances your portfolio for you or you are otherwise getting excellent service, advice and handholding, then it seems reasonable that you should want to pay a bit for it. Table 18.2 gives a few of the reasonable alternatives we have found, all of which track the Wilshire 5000.

TABLE 18.2   TOTAL MARKET ALTERNATIVES (IN NO
                  PARTICULAR ORDER)

FUND NAME	TICKER	EXPENSE RATIO
Fidelity Spartan Total Market	FSTMX	0.25%
T. Rowe Price Total Market	POMIX	0.40%
Schwab Total Stock Market	SWTIX	0.40%
Vantagepoint Broad Market Index II	VPBMX	0.27%

Fidelity, the bastion of active trading, has a core offering of cheap index funds, and customers swear by their responsive customer service. Clearly, they are hoping some investors will cross over to their lucrative (for them) active funds. T. Rowe Price is another huge and well-established firm, but its fund is a bit pricey. Schwab, primarily known as a brokerage firm, at least has one of the strongest Internet brokerage sites. Vantage-point is to be credited with very reasonable fees.

LARGE-CAP U.S. BLEND

Large-cap blend or funds that invest in both growth and value portions of an index typically follow the S&P 500. Our picks are shown in Table 18.3.

TABLE 18.3   LARGE BLEND PICKS (IN NO PARTICULAR ORDER)

FUND NAME	TICKER	EXPENSE RATIO
Bridgeway Ultra-Large 35	BRLIX	0.15%
Vanguard 500	VFINX	0.18%
USAA S&P 500	USSPX	0.18%
Fidelity Spartan 500	FSMKX	0.19%
California Invest S&P 500	SPFIX	0.20%
Dreyfus Basic S&P 500 Stock	DSPIX	0.20%
Waterhouse Dow 30	WDOWX	0.25%
DFA Enhanced U.S. Large Company +	DFELX	0.40%
DFA U.S. Large Company +	DFLCX	0.15%
Summit Apex S&P 500	SAPIX	0.48%
Summit Apex Total Social Impact	SATSX	0.75%
SPDR 500*	SPY	0.12%
Fortune 500 Index Fund*	FFF	0.20%
Diamonds Trust Series I*	DIA	0.18%
iShares Russell 1000*	IWB	0.15%

*exchange-traded funds, involves brokerage transaction fees
+ advisor-sold fund

Barclays' iShares S&P 500 ETF can be bought and held by the small investor for a breathtakingly low annual fee, but don't ignore Vanguard's very reasonable S&P 500 mutual fund. If you have $250,000 or more, you can also choose the Admiral version of the fund. The SPDR is the most popular ETF in the world and quite reasonably priced. Other fine funds of note include the Bridgeway Ultra-large 35 index fund, which concentrates the investor into the very largest companies but provides enough components for diversification from single-company risk. It is the cheapest offering on the list, and it should be since it trades relatively few highly liquid stocks.

The Summit Total Social Impact fund is an S&P 500 fund that weights firms according to their Total Social Impact weighting, a proprietary scale rating each firm on its social responsibility. As can be seen from their fees, avoiding sin isn't free, though! The *Fortune* 500 Index Fund tracks the index of that name, which is based more on revenue than market valuation. It tends to downplay speculative tech firms, a notable weakness of the S&P 500. The Diamonds follow the Dow Jones Industrials, which is a conservative list of firms representing old-economy firms. An exceptionally cheap version in mutual fund form is the Waterhouse Dow 30 fund. A relatively diversified play at a great price is found in the iShares Russell 1000 ETF.

LARGE-CAP GROWTH

During the late 1990s advisors argued on IndexFunds.com (correctly as it turned out) that the S&P 500 was itself a growth index, not really a blend. However, things have equalized somewhat in the first few years of the 2000s so that older industrial firms have become a larger percentage while technology is less so. Our picks for this segment are shown in Table 18.4.

In this asset class, the top funds all have very competitive pricing, either in mutual fund or ETF form. We think it's primarily an issue of picking the appropriate index.

The Nasdaq-100 QQQ is an interesting animal. Although ostensibly a total market ETF representing the largest 100 stocks traded through the Nasdaq stock exchange, it is full of technology firms. Microsoft, Oracle, and other high fliers dominate. It took quite a beating in 2000 and 2001

TABLE 18.4 | **LARGE GROWTH PICKS (IN NO PARTICULAR ORDER)**

FUND NAME	TICKER	EXPENSE RATIO
Vanguard Growth Index	VIGRX	0.22%
streetTRACKS Dow Jones Large Cap Growth*	ELG	0.20%
iShares Russell 1000 Growth*	IWF	0.20%
iShares S&P 500/Barra Growth*	IVW	0.18%

*exchange-traded fund, involves brokerage transaction fees

and is still quite volatile, but perhaps it is the most liquid fund because of its high volume and also the most versatile fund because of its healthy options market. It is one of the few funds from which one can take profits by selling covered calls and still retain the underlying equity position.

LARGE-CAP VALUE

Our picks for this area are shown in Table 18.5.

As with large-cap growth, pricing is very comparable, and a closer look at the underlying index is probably called for.

MID-CAP BLEND

Our picks are shown in Table 18.6. There aren't that many offerings in the mid-cap area. Probably the most popular ETF is the Mid-Cap SPDR.

TABLE 18.5 **LARGE VALUE PICKS (IN NO PARTICULAR ORDER)**

FUND NAME	TICKER	EXPENSE RATIO
Vanguard Value Index	VIVAX	0.22%
streetTRACKS Dow Jones Large Cap Value*	ELV	0.20%
iShares Russell 1000 Value*	IWD	0.20%
iShares S&P 500/Barra Value*	IVE	0.18%

*exchange-traded fund, involves brokerage transaction fees

TABLE 18.6   MID BLEND PICKS (IN NO PARTICULAR ORDER)

FUND NAME	TICKER	EXPENSE RATIO
Fidelity Spartan Extended Market	FSEMX	0.24%
Vanguard Mid Cap	VIMSX	0.25%
Vanguard Extended Market	VEXMX	0.25%
T. Rowe Price Extended Market	PEXMX	0.40%
California Invmt S&P MidCap	SPMIX	0.40%
Dreyfus MidCap	PESPX	0.50%
Federated Mid-Cap	FMDCX	0.58%
Summit Apex S&P 400 Midcap	SAMCX	0.60%
iShares Russell Midcap*	IWR	0.20%
iShares S&P MidCap 400*	IJH	0.20%
MidCap SPDRs*	MDY	0.25%
Extended Market VIPERs*	VXF	0.20%

*exchange-traded fund, involves brokerage transaction fees

Minimum investments of $15,000 and $25,000 will keep some investors out of Fidelity Spartan and Federated Mid-Cap, respectively.

MID-CAP GROWTH

The pickings are slim in the mid-cap growth arena because index advisors are neither excited about mid-caps as a class nor about growth in general. The two funds we recommend are both ETFs, as shown in Table 18.7.

TABLE 18.7   MID GROWTH PICKS (IN NO PARTICULAR ORDER)

FUND NAME	TICKER	EXPENSE RATIO
iShares Russell Midcap Growth*	IWP	0.25%
iShares S&P MidCap 400/Barra Growth*	IJK	0.25%

*exchange-traded fund, involves brokerage transaction fees

TABLE 18.8   MID VALUE PICKS (IN NO PARTICULAR ORDER)

FUND NAME	TICKER	EXPENSE RATIO
DFA Tax-Managed US Market Val+	DTMMX	0.50%
DFA U.S. Large Cap Value+	DFLVX	0.33%
DFA U.S. Large Cap Value II+	DFCVX	0.40%
DFA U.S. Large Cap Value III+	DFUVX	0.20%
iShares Russell Midcap Value*	IWS	0.25%
iShares S&P MidCap 400/Barra Value*	IJJ	0.25%

*exchange-traded fund, involves brokerage transaction fees
+advisor-sold fund

MID-CAP VALUE

Recommended mid-cap value funds mirror their mid-cap growth siblings, plus a few additions (see Table 18.8).

SMALL-CAP BLEND

In small caps, the main index division is between the Russell 2000 and the S&P 600. As of 2002, the S&P 600 looked like the smart play. The entire list of recommended offerings appears in Table 18.9.

SMALL-CAP GROWTH

Loved by active managers and shunned by indexers, the small-cap growth sector nonetheless has a handful of excellent index fund vehicles for the interested investor (see Table 18.10).

SMALL-CAP VALUE

For many advanced indexers, this is the sweet spot when complementing large caps. They feel it brings diversification and high returns at modest risk. Our picks include those contained in Table 18.11.

TABLE 18.9   SMALL BLEND PICKS (IN NO PARTICULAR ORDER)

FUND NAME	TICKER	EXPENSE RATIO
iShares Russell 2000*	IWM	0.20%
IShares S&P SmallCap 600*	IJR	0.20%
Vanguard Small Cap	NAESX	0.27%
Galaxy II Small Index	ISCIX	0.41%
DFA U.S. Micro Cap +	DFSCX	0.56%
DFA U.S. Small Cap +	DFSTX	0.43%
Schwab Small Cap	SWSMX	0.49%
Merrill Lynch Small Cap A	MASKX	0.50%
Northern Small Cap	NSIDX	0.65%
E*TRADE Russell 2000 Index	ETRUX	0.65%
California Investment S&P SmallCap	SMCIX	0.65%
Summit Apex Russell 2000	SARSX	0.75%

*exchange-traded fund, involves brokerage transaction fees
+advisor-sold fund

TABLE 18.10   SMALL GROWTH PICKS (IN NO PARTICULAR ORDER)

FUND NAME	TICKER	EXPENSE RATIO
Vanguard Small Cap Growth	VISGX	0.27%
Dreyfus Small Cap Stock	DISSX	0.50%
streetTRACKS Dow Jones Small Cap Growth*	DSG	0.25%
iShares Russell 2000 Growth*	IWO	0.25%
iShares S&P SmallCap 600/Barra Growth*	IJT	0.25%

*exchange-traded fund, involves brokerage transaction fees

TABLE 18.11   SMALL VALUE PICKS (IN NO PARTICULAR
ORDER)

FUND NAME	TICKER	EXPENSE RATIO
Vanguard Small Cap Value	VISVX	0.27%
DFA Tax-Managed U.S. Small Cap[†]	DFTSX	0.61%
DFA Tax-Mgd U.S. Small Cap Value[†]	DTMVX	0.60%
DFA U.S. 6–10 Value II[†]	DFAVX	0.42%
DFA U.S. Small Cap Value[†]	DFSVX	0.56%
Bridgeway Ultra-Small	BRSIX	0.75%
streetTRACKS Dow Jones Small Cap Value[*]	DSV	0.25%
iShares Russell 2000 Value[*]	IWN	0.25%
iShares S&P SmallCap 600/Barra Value[*]	IJS	0.25%

[*]exchange-traded fund, involves brokerage transaction fees
[†]advisor-sold fund

INTERNATIONAL

As with domestic total market indexes, our view of international is that
one should start with total market products for the portion of the portfolio that is likely to remain unchanged. Our top picks for exposure to non-
U.S. stocks in major industrial stock markets include those shown in
Table 18.12.

TABLE 18.12   TOP INTERNATIONAL (IN NO PARTICULAR ORDER)

FUND NAME	TICKER	EXPENSE RATIO
Vanguard Tax-Managed International	VTMGX	0.35%
Vanguard Developed Markets Index	VDMIX	0.32%
[*]iShares MSCI EAFE Index Fund	EFA	0.35%

[*]exchange-traded fund, involves brokerage transaction fees

TABLE 18.13   OTHER INTERNATIONAL (IN NO PARTICULAR
                     ORDER)

FUND NAME	TICKER	EXPENSE RATIO
Vantagepoint Overseas II	VPOEX	0.48%
Summit EAFE International Index Fund	SAEIX	1.25%
Merrill Lynch International Index D	MDIIX	0.89%
Fidelity Spartan International Index	FSIIX	0.35%
Eclipse EAFE Index	NIEAX	0.94%
E*TRADE International Index	ETINX	0.65%
Dreyfus International Stock Index	DIISX	0.60%
TIAA-CREF International Equity	TIINX	0.49%

Surprise! It's Vanguard and Barclays for a change. Yes, it does get a bit repetitive, but there it is. All of them track the EAFE index. As usual, Vanguard has the strongest mutual fund, whereas Barclays is applying pressure with its ETF. We also are quite happy to recommend a number of other mostly EAFE funds with slightly higher fees (see Table 18.13).

INTERNATIONAL GROWTH AND VALUE

Table 18.14 shows a handful of fine growth and value funds that span major non-U.S. markets to help an investor overweight in either direction.

TABLE 18.14   INTERNATIONAL STYLE (IN NO PARTICULAR ORDER)

FUND NAME	TICKER	EXPENSE RATIO
Vanguard International Growth Fund	VWIGX	0.81%
Vanguard International Value	VTRIX	0.64%
DFA International Value III†	DFIX	0.33%

†advisor-sold fund

TABLE 18.15   REGIONAL FUNDS (IN NO PARTICULAR ORDER)

FUND NAME	TICKER	EXPENSE F REGION
Vanguard Pacific Stock Index	VPACX	0.37 Pacific
Waterhouse Asian Index	TDASX	0.58 Pacific
*iShares MSCI Pacific ex-Japan	EPP	0.50 Pacific
Waterhouse European Index	TDEUX	0.58 Europe Stock
Vanguard Euro Stock Index	VEURX	0.34 Europe Stock
*iShares S&P Europe 350 Index	IEV	0.60 Europe Stock
*iShares S&P Latin America 40 Index	ILF	0.50 Latin America Stock

*exchange-traded fund, involves brokerage transaction fees

REGIONAL FUNDS

For the first round of geographic precision in international indexing we recommend regional funds. The most common strategies for investors here is to overweight Europe when the United States seems especially pricey or to underweight Japan if it still appears to have lingering economic stagnation and stock overvaluation. The funds that invest in large companies are well priced (see Table 18.15).

EMERGING MARKET FUNDS

Emerging market funds provide a little extra kick but with plenty of risk. However, they also bring relative lack of correlation with the United States. Some funds we recommend are shown in Table 18.16.

TABLE 18.16   EMERGING MARKETS (IN NO PARTICULAR ORDER)

FUND NAME	TICKER	EXPENSE RATIO
Vanguard Emerging Markets Stock Index	VEIEX	0.60
DFA Emerging Markets Portfolio	DFEMX	0.90

Country Funds

Placing bets on one or two individual countries is not highly recommended unless the investor really has insight into that market. It makes sense if one country in particular trails regional peers and traditionally has kept up with them. Keep in mind that these funds are relatively expensive, so holding quite a few of them at once is wasteful. It is better to stick with regional funds. Still, these ETFs are solid offerings and let the investor get in and out quickly (Table 18.17).

Bond Funds

As we have said previously, bonds are an absolute no-brainer to index. Active management historically provides very little potential upside in the investment-grade area. There are no Peter Lynch's of the bond market! Recall that we primarily recommend short-term bonds for their lack of correlation to the stock market and for their low risk. Our picks for short-, intermediate-, and long-term bonds appear in Table 18.18.

Keep in mind that you can always call Uncle Sam and buy some Treasury bonds directly. It doesn't get safer than that.

Sector Funds

For those individuals with a very strong hunch about an industrial sector, there are dozens of perfectly adequate indexed funds and ETFs. As with choosing individual countries, we feel this exercise is best left to those individuals who really know the industry well. The funds do tend to be expensive, and they do concentrate one in a relatively small number of stocks.

The large industrial category SPDRs are quite reasonably priced and not so concentrated. They may prove useful in hedges against perceived bubbles in parts of the economy. For the determined sector investor, there are many more alternatives, many quite reasonably priced (see Table 18.19).

TABLE 18.17   COUNTRY FUNDS (IN NO PARTICULAR ORDER)

FUND NAME	TICKER	EXPENSE RATIO
*iShares S&P/TOPIX 150 Index	ITF	0.50
*iShares MSCI Japan Index	EWJ	0.84
*iShares MSCI Taiwan Index	EWT	0.99
*iShares MSCI South Korea Index	EWY	0.99
*iShares MSCI Singapore (Free) Index	EWS	0.84
*iShares MSCI Malaysia (Free) Index	EWM	0.84
*iShares MSCI Hong Kong Index	EWH	0.84
*iShares MSCI United Kingdom Index	EWU	0.84
*iShares MSCI Switzerland Index	EWL	0.84
*iShares MSCI Sweden Index	EWD	0.84
*iShares MSCI Spain Index	EWP	0.84
*iShares MSCI Netherlands Index	EWN	0.84
*iShares MSCI Italy Index	EWI	0.84
*iShares MSCI Germany Index	EWG	0.84
*iShares MSCI France Index	EWQ	0.84
*iShares MSCI EMU Index	EZU	0.84
*iShares MSCI Belgium Index	EWK	0.84
*iShares MSCI Austria Index	EWO	0.84
*iShares MSCI Brazil (Free) Index	EWZ	0.99
*iShares MSCI Mexico (Free) Index	EWW	0.84
*iShares S&P/TSE 60 Index	IKC	0.50
*iShares MSCI Canada Index	EWC	0.84
*iShares MSCI Australia Index	EWA	0.84

*exchange-traded fund, involves brokerage transaction fees

TABLE 18.18   BONDS (IN NO PARTICULAR ORDER)

FUND NAME	TICKER	EXPENSE RATIO
Short-Term Bonds		
Vanguard Short-Term Bond Index	VBISX	0.21
Schwab Short-Term Bond Market Index	SWBDX	0.35
Intermediate-Term Bonds		
Vanguard Total Bond Index	VBMFX	0.22
Vanguard Intm Bond Index	VBIIX	0.21
Summit Lehman Bond Index Fund	SALAX	0.60
Schwab Total Bond Market Index	SWLBX	0.35
E*TRADE Bond	ETBDX	0.65
Dreyfus Bond Market Index Inv	DBMIX	0.40
Long-Term Bonds		
Vanguard Long-Term Bond Index	VBLTX	0.21
Eclipse Indexed Bond	NIIBX	0.50

We really like HOLDRs as an inexpensive way to target particular industries, with the caveat that their composition does not change.

FUND GROUPS

Funds are a reflection of their creators, and we think the following fund groups add originality and value in their offerings and may offer insight into their operations.

BARCLAYS GLOBAL INVESTORS

Not many individual U.S. investors had heard of this firm before it ramped up its iShares line of global ETFs in the late 1990s. Still, it is considered the largest manager of index funds in the world. Until recent years

TABLE 18.19   DOMESTIC SECTORS (IN NO PARTICULAR ORDER)

FUND NAME	TICKER	EXPENSE RATIO
State Street ETFs		
Basic Industries Select Sector SPDR	XLB	0.27
Consumer Services Select Sector SPDR	XLV	0.28
Consumer Staples Select Sector SPDR	XLP	0.28
Cyclical/Transportation Select SPDR	XLY	0.27
Energy Select Sector SPDR	XLE	0.28
Financial Select Sector SPDR	XLF	0.27
Industrial Select Sector SPDR	XLI	0.28
Technology Select Sector SPDR	XLK	0.28
Utilities Select Sector SPDR	XLU	0.29
streetTRACKS Morgan Stanley HighTech	MTK	0.51
streetTRACKS Morgan Stanley High Internet	MII	0.53
streetTRACKS Wilshire REIT Fund	RWR	0.32
Fortune e-50 Index	FEF	0.22
Barclays ETFs		
iShares Cohen & Steers Realty Majors	ICF	0.35
iShares Dow Jones US Basic Materials	IYM	0.60
iShares Dow Jones US Chemicals	IYD	0.60
iShares Dow Jones US Cons Non-Cycl	IYK	0.60
iShares Dow Jones US Consumer Cycl	IYC	0.60
iShares Dow Jones US Energy	IYE	0.60
iShares Dow Jones US Financial Sector	IYF	0.60
iShares Dow Jones US Financial Svcs	IYG	0.60
iShares Dow Jones US Healthcare	IYH	0.60
iShares Dow Jones US Industrial	IYJ	0.60
iShares Dow Jones US Internet	IYV	0.60
iShares Dow Jones US Real Estate	IYR	0.60
iShares Dow Jones US Technology	IYW	0.60
iShares Dow Jones US Telecom	IYZ	0.60
iShares Dow Jones US Utilities	IDU	0.60
iShares Goldman Sachs Natural Resources	IGE	0.50

TABLE 18.19   (CONTINUED)

FUND NAME	TICKER	EXPENSE RATIO
Barclays ETFs (*Continued*)		
iShares Goldman Sachs Networking	IGN	0.50
iShares Goldman Sachs Semiconductor	IGW	0.50
iShares Goldman Sachs Software Index	IGV	0.50
iShares Goldman Sachs Technology Index	IGM	0.50
iShares Nasdaq Biotechnology	IBB	0.50
Vanguard Sector Index Funds		
Vanguard Energy Fund	VGENX	0.39
Vanguard Health Care	VGHCX	0.31
Vanguard Precious Metals	VGPMX	0.63
Vanguard REIT	VGSIX	0.28
Vanguard Utilities Income	VGSUX	0.37
HOLDRs		
Biotech HOLDRs*	BBH	0.60
Broadband HOLDRs*	BDH	0.60
B2B Interet HOLDRs*	BHH	0.60
Europe 2001 HOLDRs*	EKH	0.60
Internet HOLDRs*	HHH	0.60
Internet Architecture HOLDRs*	IAH	0.60
Internet Infrastructure HOLDRs*	IIH	0.60
Market 2000+ HOLDRs*	MKH	0.60
Oil Services HOLDRs*	OIH	0.60
Pharmaceutical HOLDRs*	PPH	0.60
Regional Bank HOLDRs*	RKH	0.60
Retail HOLDRs*	RTH	0.60
Semiconductor HOLDRs*	SMH	0.60
Software HOLDRs*	SWH	0.60
Telecom HOLDRs*	TTH	0.60
Utilities HOLDRs*	UTH	0.60
Wireless HOLDRs*	WMH	0.60

*annual custody fee of 0.08% is charged if any of the underlying stocks pay dividends.

it has concentrated on the institutional market. A spin-off of the venerable English bank, Barclays Global Investors handles equities all over the world. It is headquartered in San Francisco. The launch of its iShares ETFs is a major foray into the retail index fund market, and the firm has spent heavily advertising and marketing the funds.

BRIDGEWAY CAPITAL MANAGEMENT

Bridgeway Capital Management is a small and unique fund shop founded in 1993 by John Montgomery. Montgomery began as a research engineer at MIT but became interested in applying quantitative computer models to the stock market and received an MBA from Harvard University in 1985. Bridgeway funds have very low expense ratios and high tax efficiency, and Montgomery is respected by many industry observers for his integrity and straightforward shareholder letters. Bridgeway funds charge a management fee based on performance, which tends to align the interests of the fund manager and shareholders. For example, Bridgeway is quicker than most shops to close funds to new cash because performance is so important. Bridgeway is able to slash costs because it is a quantitative shop and doesn't pay for outside research or analysts; also, the firm pays for all of its own fund distribution costs. The firm is headquartered at modest offices in Houston, Texas. Bridgeway offers some unique index funds. The Bridgeway Ultra-Large 35 Index is an equal-weighted index of 35 large companies. The fund has correlated strongly with the S&P 500 and has a razor-thin expense ratio at 0.15%. At the other end of the spectrum, the Bridgeway Ultra-Small Company Index is a great choice for indexers seeking exposure to extremely small and deep value companies.

DIMENSIONAL FUND ADVISORS

This quirky and brilliant fund group has a very strong following among many index advisors. It offers a wide array of basic U.S. asset classes as well as international ones, but its passion and strength appear to be in the value and small-cap asset classes. Although this strategy is by no means unique, its traders are renowned for their optimization strategies. They regularly beat listed indexes of small-cap and international stocks by sampling and other techniques. For instance, they will put out the word generally that they have a list of illiquid firms in which they are willing to buy relatively large blocks of stock at below-market prices. Because the sellers fear an open offer to buy so much stock would depress the price far more, they often agree to the small discount for a quiet trade. DFA advisors appear to believe thoroughly that value in U.S. equities will offer higher returns long term than growth.

DFA's small value funds are considered to be the best of their breed by many. For the average investor, this asset class may be overweighted quite reasonably, but it is not likely to exceed 20% in most portfolios.

The problem with DFA is that they are so secretive. They communicate with their investors far less than other fund groups, preferring instead to let advisors explain their offerings and strategies. We are told that even with their advisors they are quite tight-lipped. There is no way for an investor without millions of dollars on hand to invest with DFA without going through one of their approved advisors. They are essentially gatekeepers, and in our view they are in some cases extracting fees that don't necessarily reflect their value added. Many such advisors charge nontrivial fees of 0.5% of assets per year and more that are only gradually reduced for larger clients. On the other hand, several DFA advisors proudly advertise their willingness to take 0.25% of assets per year, so it is possible to work through an advisor at reasonable cost.

We are not aware of any unbiased study of what a reasonable cost for advice should be. The laws of compounding interest must weigh heavily upon any such fee. It needs to be justified, given the many fine options for direct investment available to the investor, and it can be easily, in our view, up to about 0.5% of assets in annual fees per year. Above that investors really need to ask whether they are requesting more service than they need.

DFA makes sense for the individual who has at least $500,000 to invest, already wants to hire an advisor anyway, and doesn't mind the firm's eccentricities. Otherwise, DFA is probably not appropriate for the average individual, as I believe the value of a possibly superior small value or international fund is largely undone by their insistence on an advisor.

In addition, most curious investors will find their closed-mouth communications policies annoying.

STATE STREET ADVISORS

This firm manages the SPDR, largest ETF in the United States, along with index provider Standard & Poor's. It has deep experience in money management and is known for quiet competence but not necessarily innovation.

SUMMIT

Summit is a small index fund group with eight index funds covering the bases of U.S. investing. Summit also has an MSCI EAFE index fund for broad international diversification. Summit is a relatively new player on the index scene; three years ago Union Central Life Insurance spun off its investments department to create Summit. Summit's index funds don't have the economy of scale of Vanguard index funds, but the average fund holds $25 billion in assets, according to management. Therefore, Summit's index funds have higher expense ratios when compared to the Vanguard funds. However, Summit is not attempting to undercut the expense ratios of the bigger competing funds. Rather, its goal is to target small and mid size financial intermediaries that may be ignored by the bigger players for lack of assets.

The firm is committed to indexing, and one of its major goals is educate investors and advisors on the benefits of low-cost index funds. Summit offers the unique socially responsible Total Social Impact Fund. The TSI Fund invests in all of the stocks in the S&P 500, but it weights the companies differently according to their Total Social Impact rating. The rating reflects the company's scoring on a series of benchmarks corresponding to each of its stakeholders, created by the *Caux Principles*, a statement of business ethics developed by international corporate leaders.

VANGUARD GROUP

Indexing wouldn't be available to the individual investor to any degree without the Vanguard Group. It was the pioneer of index mutual funds and is still remarkable in its tenacious pursuit of the index investor's interests. It never tried to cash in on its success by changing its tune. It has both active and index funds totaling $550 billion.

It is very much a reflection of founder John C. Bogle, who in 1949 wrote his senior thesis as an undergraduate at Princeton University on index investing. He has been putting the idea into practice ever since. He spent some disillusioned years at an active mutual fund company and followed closely the "random walk" ideas of Burton Malkiel and other academics. His first principle has been to keep all offerings as inexpensive as possible.

Finally, in 1975 he founded the Vanguard Group, and Vanguard obtained licensing rights to the struggling S&P 500 Index for a song and to this day pays a pittance for the right to track it and use its name. (The S&P lawsuit mentioned earlier is a result of the licensing fees that heavily favored Vanguard.) The mutual fund industry mocked him and dubbed the endeavor "Bogle's Folly." However, Bogle had the last laugh when the offering grew and prospered, and it is poised to become the largest fund in the world. John J. Brennan, who joined Vanguard in 1982, replaced Bogle as CEO in 1986, but Bogle still keeps an office at the Vanguard headquarters and speaks at conferences and appears on television frequently. Bogle has remained an active mutual fund shareholder even in retirement. Most recently, he has spoken out against the corporate governance and accounting practices that led to the Enron debacle.

Vanguard is organized in a unique manner. It is literally owned by the investors in its funds. Even if the group did charge high fees, any excess profits would have to be returned to the shareholder/investors. Vanguard has innovated on numerous fronts, including optimization strategies for sticking close to indexes without incurring excessive transaction costs. Vanguard's fund managers have been given the flexibility to use hedging and sampling strategies to track benchmarks closely but not slavishly. The result is that they often pick up a few tenths of a percentage in performance each year over what they would have if they had mechanically followed the index. The group also introduced special fund versions for low tax impacts and offers volume discounts in their Admiral line of funds for high-net worth individuals.

Vanguard was most notably trailing the industry when it finally introduced its Vipers line of ETFs. As mentioned in Chapter 17, S&P sued Vanguard when the group tried to launch an ETF based on the S&P 500, and Vanguard promptly retracted its application before the Securities Exchange Commission rather than pay extra licensing fees. No firm has delivered more value for the dollar over years than Vanguard, and this firm seems as intent as ever to work hard on behalf of the indexer as opposed to lining its own pockets. However, it's not what you did for me yesterday that counts, it's what you are going to do for me today and even tomorrow!

CHAPTER 19

Track, Rebalance, and Reassess

To know how one's portfolio has performed is the first order of business. Information about how your portfolio did on an annualized basis is usually provided in a straightforward manner by reputable firms. If you have the value of net assets of your portfolio in the beginning of the year and the end, it's simple arithmetic to calculate your return:

Percentage return = (ending value / starting value) − 1

This assumes that all dividends are reinvested in each fund so there is no cash interest leaving it. In this case the average is the annualized amount. If the time period is longer than one year, the following steps will deliver an annualized return:

1. Obtain your total percentage return as above.
2. $x = ((\% \text{ return } /100) + 1) \times 1 / (\text{total \# days } /365)$
3. Annualized performance = $(x - 1) \times 100$

At this point you should have the tools to know how your various funds have performed over any time period.

REBALANCING

Like the wind, every index turns in unpredictable ways. If index investors wish to stay true to their original path, they should rebalance at reasonable intervals. Rebalancing is the practice of selling part of your indexes that have done well to buy those that have done less well to maintain the original asset allocation strategy. Most investors would like to keep a constant ratio between these assets so that they don't end up with a more risky or lesser performance potential than they originally intended. However, because different asset classes perform differently during the year, the need to rebalance arises.

Consider a portfolio composed in 1995 of equal parts government Treasury bonds, the S&P 500, and international stocks. Over time this portfolio will begin to look lopsided, as stocks and especially U.S. stocks surge, leaving bonds far behind (see Table 19.1).

Soon the asset allocations fall out of line with their targets.

Recall the old adage "Buy low and sell high." Here the winners are "high" and the losers "low" in terms of their percentage of the entire portfolio relative to where they started the period. Rebalancing is, in effect, a systematic way to force the sale of assets that have surged in order to buy ones that have lagged. Why on earth would you sell the winners to buy the losers? For the same reasons that you believe in indexing in the first place:

- Reversion to the mean

- Long-term horizon

- Steady risk profile

- Diversification

Recall that reversion to the mean suggests that high returns for an asset are not likely to be sustained. They are likely to return to the histor-

TABLE 19.1   ASSET ALLOCATION PERCENTAGES OVER TIME

	S&P 500	MSCI EAFE	TREASURY BOND	
1995 return	37.43%	11.63%	14.40%	
1996 return	23.07%	6.23%	3.99%	
1997 return	33.37%	2.02%	7.69%	
1998 return	28.58%	20.25%	8.62%	
1999 return	21.03%	27.27%	0.40%	
2000 return	−9.10%	−13.95%	10.25%	
2001 return	−11.88%	−21.21%	8.16%	
UN-REBALANCED	S&P 500	MSCI EAFE	TREASURY BOND	TOTAL
1995 return	137.43%	111.63%	114.40%	**363.46%**
1996 return	169.14%	118.58%	118.96%	**406.68%**
1997 return	225.58%	120.98%	128.11%	**474.67%**
1998 return	290.04%	145.48%	139.16%	**574.68%**
1999 return	351.04%	185.15%	139.71%	**675.90%**
2000 return	319.10%	159.32%	154.03%	**632.45%**
2001 return	281.19%	125.53%	166.60%	**573.32%**
Start	100	100	100	**300**
Rate	15.92%	3.30%	7.56%	
REBALANCED	S&P 500	MSCI EAFE	TREASURY BOND	TOTAL
1995 return	137.43%	111.63%	114.40%	**363.46%**
1996 return	149.10%	128.70%	125.99%	**403.79%**
1997 return	179.51%	137.32%	144.95%	**461.78%**
1998 return	197.92%	185.10%	167.19%	**550.21%**
1999 return	221.97%	233.42%	184.14%	**639.52%**
2000 return	193.78%	183.44%	235.02%	**612.24%**
2001 return	179.83%	160.79%	220.73%	**561.36%**
Start				**300**

TABLE 19.1 (CONTINUED)

	NON-REBALANCED PORTFOLIO	REBALANCED PORTFOLIO
1995 return	21.15%	21.15%
1996 return	11.89%	11.10%
1997 return	16.72%	14.36%
1998 return	21.07%	19.15%
1999 return	17.61%	16.23%
2000 return	−6.43%	−4.27%
2001 return	−9.35%	−8.31%
1995–2001	9.69%	9.36%
STD DEV.	12.89%	11.59%

SOURCE: Morningstar data

ical mean. The more they have exceeded the historical mean, the more likely they are to return there quickly (fall).

A long-term horizon removes the temptation to chase a temporary momentum play. Sure, a popular asset may continue to spike, but the investor's entire outlook is over many years, during which time the current trends will appear as a blip on the screen.

The index investor seeks a steady risk profile and recognizes that the more an asset becomes the center of attention among day-traders and momentum investors, the more its risk is likely to go up. In terms of its risk profile the S&P 500 at the top of the equity bubble in the late 1990s simply wasn't the same asset as earlier in the decade. Returns to the investor were higher, and the subsequent price per current dollar of earnings was far higher to reflect optimism about continuing high rates of growth. Even if the companies had continued to grow their profits quickly and merit their high valuations, the implication would have been the same: Those stocks were simply not offering the same risk/reward profile as they were before.

For these and probably many other reasons most indexing observers find it prudent to lock in some of the gains by returning the portfolio to

FIGURE 19.1   GRAPH OF THE TWO PORTFOLIOS

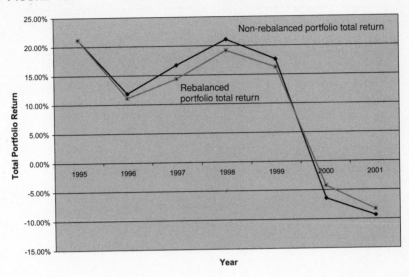

its original asset allocation percentages. According to Paul Samuelson, "That's a great way of controlling risk as against what is in effect pyramiding or letting your gains run."[1]

In Figure 19.1 we compare the investor with equal parts bonds, S&P, and international stocks who rebalances every year from 1995 through 2002 versus an investor with the same portfolio who does not.

There is a cost to rebalance, so doing it at moderate intervals is recommended. This is why indexers often don't bother until an asset class is 5% or so off its target percentage. Over time the general trend is for equities to outstrip bonds, but sometimes this may take years and there will be little dips and hills along the way. There is no need to get involved unless the amounts are substantial.

For portfolios where new cash is still being invested, the most elegant way of rebalancing may be obtained by placing all that new money in the laggard asset classes.

For the portfolio with no new inputs, selling one asset to buy another may be necessary. Selling covered calls with ETFs is another way to obtain a similar effect.

Glossary

ALPHA Measure of performance in percentage above or below what would have been predicted by risk as suggested by its beta. A positive alpha means a fund performed better than its risk would suggest, whereas a negative alpha means the fund underperformed. An ETF of alpha 1.5 outperformed its index by 1.5% as predicted by its beta.

ANNUAL TURNOVER Percentage of a portfolio that is replaced each year.

ASSET CLASS BREAKDOWN Percentage of holdings in different types of investments.

BALANCED FUNDS Funds that invest in both stocks and bonds.

BENCHMARK INDEX Index that correlates with a fund; used to measure a fund manager's performance.

BETA Measure of volatility. Beta is a fund's volatility measured against the benchmark index, which has a set beta of 1. Therefore, if a fund has a beta higher than 1, it is moving up and down more than the rest of the market. A fund with a beta of 2 will move up 20% when the market rises 10%.

CAPITAL GAINS Taxable profits on the sale of stocks.

CLOSET INDEX FUND Active fund with higher fees that simply tracks an index.

DEFERRED LOAD Percentage of an investor's assets that a fund may charge as a fee at time of redemption.

DIVIDEND YIELD Company's declared dividends per share as a percentage of its current share price.

DOLLAR COST AVERAGING Investment strategy of making fixed investments (monthly, for example) to a mutual fund.

ENHANCED INDEX FUND Index fund that is designed to generally track an index but also to outperform it through the use of futures, trading strategy, capital gains management, and other methods.

EXCHANGE-TRADED FUND Index fund that is traded on the stock market. Some common ETFs are the Nasdaq-100 Index Tracking Stock (QQQ), which tracks the Nasdaq 100, and Standard & Poor's Depositary Receipts (SPY), which tracks the S&P 500.

EXPENSE RATIO The percentage of fund assets that a fund manager may withdraw each year to pay for operating expenses.

FLOAT Number of company shares actually available for purchase by the public on open markets.

FRONT LOAD Percentage of an investor's assets that a fund may charge as a fee at the time of investment.

GROWTH STOCK Companies that grow earnings and revenues faster than other companies in their economic sector or the market as a whole. Growth companies tend to pay little or no dividends, opting to spend profits on further expansion.

INDEX FUND Mutual fund that mirrors as closely as possible the performance of a stock market index. For example, many mutual fund companies have since established S&P 500 Index funds to mirror that index by purchasing all 500 stocks in the same percentages as the index.

INDEXING Investment strategy to match the average performance of a market or group of stocks. Usually, this is accomplished by buying a small amount of each stock in a market. An index, such as the S&P 500, represents the market or group of stocks.

LARGE-CAP COMPANY Stocks with a relatively large market capitalization, as measured by company stock price multiplied by total shares outstanding. Large-cap companies generally have a market capitalization between $10 billion and $200 billion.

MARKET CAPITALIZATION Total value of a company; total number of shares multiplied by the price of a share.

MID-CAP COMPANY Stocks with a "middle" market capitalization, as measured by company stock price multiplied by total shares outstanding. Mid-cap stocks generally have a market capitalization between $2 billion to $10 billion.

MINIMUM INITIAL PURCHASE Minimum an investor may deposit initially (may be lower in some cases for IRA retirement accounts).

P/B RATIO Ratio of price to book value of a stock, or average of a portfolio of stocks.

P/E RATIO Ratio of price to annualized earnings of a stock, or average of portfolio of stocks.

R SQUARED Measurement of how closely a fund's performance correlates with an index. It can range between 0.00 and 1.00. An R Squared of 1.00 indicates perfect correlation, whereas an R Squared of 0.00 indicates no correlation.

RETURNS Total percentage gain of a fund over a time period.

SECTOR BREAKDOWN Percentage of a fund's equity holdings in various industries.

SECURITIES AND EXCHANGE COMMISSION Federal agency that regulates U.S. financial markets, also known as SEC.

SHARPE RATIO THREE YEAR Risk-adjusted measurement of fund performance. The Sharpe ratio is calculated by dividing the excess return of a fund over the risk-free rate by its standard deviation. The higher the Sharpe ratio, the better a fund's risk-adjusted performance.

SMALL-CAP COMPANY Stocks with a relatively small market capitalization, as measured by company stock price multiplied by total shares outstanding. Small-cap companies generally have a market capitalization between $300 million to $2 billion.

STANDARD DEVIATION THREE YEAR Measure of fund volatility in percentages. Standard deviation measures the average variability of the fund's returns over a time period. Stable investments like money market funds have standard deviations near zero, while high-risk equity funds often have much higher ones. A standard deviation of 10 means approximately 68% of the time a fund will be within 10% of its mean (average) price.

STYLE DRIFT When a fund moves away from its stated investment objective over time.

THREE-YEAR EARNINGS GROWTH Rate of increase of earnings of past three years.

TICKER SYMBOL Symbol used by brokerage firms to identify fund.

TOTAL NET ASSETS Total amount of assets a fund holds as of a certain date.

TRACKING ERROR How much a fund's returns deviate from the benchmark index's return.

12-B1 EXPENSES Percentage of fund assets that fund manager may withdraw each year to pay for marketing and other non-operating expenses.

VALUE STOCK Companies that are considered undervalued or "cheap" relative to current stock prices. Value companies generally have low valuation measures such as price-to-book ratio. Value stocks also have attractive hard assets, strong fundamentals, and pay regular dividends. Legendary investor Warren Buffett is considered perhaps the greatest value investor of all time.

YTD The calendar year to date (that is, January 1 to the end of the last month).

Notes

Chapter 1

1. *Where Are the Customers' Yachts?* Fred Schwed, Jr. Simon & Schuster, 1940.

Chapter 2

1. *The Fortune Sellers: The Big Business of Selling and Buying Predictions.* William A. Sherden. John Wiley and Sons, 1997.
2. *The Internet Bubble.* Anthony B. Perkins and Michael C. Perkins. HarperBusiness, 2001.
3. "Beyond the Bubble: An Interview with Robert Shiller." Anne Kates Smith. Thestreet.com, April 8, 2000.
4. "Twenty Five Years of Indexing," PricewaterhouseCoopers, 1998 report.

Chapter 3

1. *The Fortune Sellers: The Big Business of Selling and Buying Predictions.* William A. Sherden. John Wiley and Sons, 1997.
2. "Expansion Waters Down Mutual Fund Industry" by Ian McDonald, *The Wall Street Journal*, April 2, 2002.

Chapter 4

1. *Where Are the Customers' Yachts?* Fred Schwed, Jr. Simon & Schuster, 1940.
2. *A Random Walk Down Wall Street.* Burton Malkiel. Norton, 1973.
3. "The "Dartboard" Column: The Pros, the Darts, and the Market" by Bing Liang, Case Western Reserve University.
4. "The "Dartboard" Column: The Pros, the Darts, and the Market", by Bing Liang, Case Western Reserve University.
5. "Stars Alone Don't Illuminate Performance Picture" by Karen Damato, *The Wall Street Journal*, March 22, 2002.
6. Morningstar's Risk-adjusted Ratings." William Sharpe. Stanford University, 1998.

Chapter 5

1. *Dow Jones Investment Advisor* article, April, 1998.
2. "Morningstar's Risk-adjusted Ratings," January 1998, William Sharpe, Stanford University.
3. "Telecom Stocks Fall, Depressing Rest of Market," *The Wall Street Journal*, April 23, 2002.
4. *The Intelligent Investor.* Benjamin Graham. Harper & Row, 1973.
5. *The Intelligent Investor.* Benjamin Graham. Harper & Row, 1973.

Chapter 6

1. *Against the Gods: The Remarkable Story of Risk.* Peter Bernstein, John Wiley and Sons, 1996.
2. "Evidence on the Speed of Convergence to Market Efficiency." Richard Roll, The John E. Anderson Graduate School of Management, UCLA. Keynote Presentation, The 6th Annual Superbowl of Indexing, December, 2001, Phoenix, Arizona.
3. "A Rose.Com by Any Other Name." Mike Cooper, Orlin Dimitrov and P. Raghavendra Rau, Krannert Graduate School of Management, Purdue University.
4. *The New Finance: The Case against Efficient Markets.* Robert A. Haugen. Prentice Hall, 1999.
5. "Problems in Measuring Portfolio Performance: An Application to Contrarian Investment Strategies," S.P Kothari and J. Shanken, Journal of Financial Economics 38 (1995).

6. "Soros' Quantum Fund Is 90% in Cash." Brett D. Fromson. Thestreet.com. May 15, 2000.

7. From speech Delivered April 26, 1994 to the MIT Department of Economics World Economy Laboratory Conference Washington, D.C.

8. "3 Lessons from Ace Investor George Soros." Victor Niederhoffer and Laurel Kenner. msn.com, March 21, 2002.

9. *Devil Take the Hindmost: A History of Financial Speculation*. Edward Chancellor. Plume, 2000.

10. *The Tipping Point*. Malcolm Gladwell. Little Brown & Company, 2000.

Chapter 7

1. *Beating the Street*. Peter Lynch. Fireside, 1994.

2. *Beating the Street*. Peter Lynch. Fireside, 1994.

3. From 2000 interview with IndexFunds.com.

4. From 1999 article on IndexFunds.com.

Chapter 8

1. "Core & Explore—An Effective Strategy for Building Your Portfolio." Article posted on Schwab Web site.

2. "On Persistence in Mutual Fund Performance." Mark Carhart. Journal of Finance, March 1997.

3. *A Random Walk Down Wall Street*. Burton Malkiel. Norton, 1973.

4. "BusinessNews Analysis: Hedge Fund Problems," *The Independent*, Auguest 12, 1999.

5. "Trading Is Hazardous to Your Wealth: The Common Stock Investment Performance of Individual Investors" Terrance Odean with Brad Barber, *Journal of Finance*, April 2002.

6. "Boys Will Be Boys: Gender, Overconfidence, and Common Stock Investment." Terrance Odean and Brad Barber, *Quarterly Journal of Economics*, February 2001, Vol. 116, No. 1, 261–292.

Chapter 9

1. "The Small-Cap-Alpha Myth." Research Paper by Index Funds Advisors, posted on Web site.

2. "Does Indexing Affect Stock Prices?" Larry Swedroe, IndexFunds. com, March 12, 2002)

Chapter 10

1. Investors Rate the Market's Risks, *The Wall Street Journal*, January 2002.
2. "The Sharpe Ratio." William Sharpe, *The Journal of Portfolio Management*, Fall 1994.
3. "The Sharpe Ratio." William Sharpe, *The Journal of Portfolio Management*, Fall 1994.
4. *Dow Jones Investment Advisor* article, April 1998.
5. *Dow Jones Investment Advisor* article, April, 1998.
6. *Valuing Wall Street*. Andrew Smithers and Stephen Wright, McGraw-Hill, 2000.

Chapter 11

1. *Stocks for the Long Run*. Jeremy J. Siegel. McGraw-Hill Professional Publishing, 1998.
2. "Move to Midcap-Stock Funds May be Timely." Bridget O'Brian, *The Wall Street Journal*, March 10, 2002.
3. "The Big Differences in Small-Stock Mutual Funds." Karen Damato, *The Wall Street Journal*, March 1, 2002)
4. "National Economies, after Fading in Unison, Hint at a Joint Upturn." Christopher Hoads and Jon Hilsenrath, *The Wall Street Journal*, March 18, 2002.

Chapter 12

1. *Beating the Street*. Peter Lynch. Fireside, 1994.
2. "Mutual Funds Load Up on Fees." Jeff Opdyke, *The Wall Street Journal*, April 10, 2002.

Chapter 15

1. "Why You Should Have No Confidence in Consumer Confidence." Deloitte & Touche Study, April 12, 2002.

2. "How Indexes Are Created: Ramifications for the Index Investor" Rahul Seksaria, IndexFunds.com, 1999.

3. *Exchange Traded Funds.* Jim Wiandt and Will McClatchy (IndexFunds.com). John Wiley and Sons, 2002

Chapter 17

1. *Exchange Traded Funds.* Jim Wiandt and Will McClatchy (IndexFunds.com). John Wiley and Sons, 2002

2. "Bogle Cautions Indexers on ETF Speculation." Will McClatchy, IndexFunds.com, December 5, 2001.

Chapter 19

1. *Dow Jones Investment Advisor* article, April, 1998.

Bibliography

Bogle, John. "Reversion to the Mean: The 'Investment Law of Gravity.'" Speech given in 1998 as related by www.Vanguard.com.

"BusinessNews Analysis: Hedge Fund Problems." *The Independent*, August, 1999.

"Calculating Annualized Returns for Group Averages." Lipper & Co., 2002.

Carhart, Mark. "On Persistence in Mutual Fund Performance." *Journal of Finance*, 1997.

Chancellor, Edward. *Devil Take the Hindmost*. Plume Books, 1999.

Clements, Jonathan. "Managed Funds Can't Match Market." *The Wall Street Journal*.

Cooper, Mike, Orlin Dimitrov, and P. Raghavendra Rau. "A Rose.Com by Any Other Name." Krannert Graduate School of Management, Purdue University.

Damato, Karen. "The Big Differences in Small-Stock Mutual Funds." *The Wall Street Journal*, March 1, 2002

Damato, Karen. "Stars Alone Don't Illuminate Performance Picture." *The Wall Street Journal*, March 22, 2002.

Farrell, Paul B. "The Death of No-Loads? Why Pay for Something You Can Get Free." CBS.MarketWatch.com, March 12, 2002.

Goetzmann, William N. "An Introduction to Investment Theory." Yale School of Management.

Graham, Benjamin. *The Intelligent Investor*. Harper & Row, 1973.

Hoads, Christopher and Jon Hilsenrath. "National Economies, After Fading in Unison, Hint at a Joint Upturn." *The Wall Street Journal*, March 18, 2002.

Lauricella, Tom. "Morningstar to Alter Classification Method", *The Wall Street Journal*, March 26, 2002

Lynch, Peter. *Beating the Street*. Fireside, 1994.

McClatchy, Will. "Bogle Cautions Indexers on ETF Speculation." IndexFunds.com, December, 2001.

McClatchy, Will. "Chaos Theorist Discusses the Markets and Nonlinear Theory." IndexFunds.com.

McClatchy, Will. "Schwab Backs Indexing." IndexFunds, March, 1999.

McClatchy, Will, John Spence, Paul Weil, and Jim Wiandt. "Waste Meter." IndexFunds.com, October, 2000.

McClatchy, Will and Jim Wiandt. *Exchange-Traded Funds*. John Wiley and Sons, 2002.

"Morningstar Study Confirms Virtues of Buy-and-Hold in Bear Market." IndexFunds Staff, March, 2002.

Niederhoffer, Victor and Laurel Kenner. "3 Lessons from Ace Investor George Soros." msn.com, March 21, 2002.

O'Brian, Bridget. "Move to Midcap-Stock Funds May Be Timely." *The Wall Street Journal*, March 10, 2002.

Odean, Terrance and Brad Barber. "Boys Will Be Boys: Gender, Overconfidence, and Common Stock Investment." *Quarterly Journal of Economics*, February 2001, Vol. 116, No. 1, 261–292.

Odean, Terrance and Brad Barber. "Trading Is Hazardous to Your Wealth: The Common Stock Investment Performance of Individual Investors." *Journal of Finance*, Vol. LV, No. 2, April, 2000.

Perkins, Anthony B and Michael C. Perkins. *The Internet Bubble*. HarperBusiness, 2001.

"Random Talks with Eugene Fama." www.Ibbotson.com, March, 2000

Samuelson, Paul. Interview with *Dow Jones Asset Management*, 1998.

Seksaria, Rahul. "How Indexes Are Created: Ramifications for the Index Investor." IndexFunds.com, 1999.

Sharpe, William F. "The Sharpe Ratio." *The Journal of Portfolio Management*, Fall 1994.

Siegel, Jeremy J. *Stocks for the Long Run*. McGraw-Hill Professional Publishing, 1998.

Smithers, Andrew and Stephen Wright. *Valuing Wall Street*. McGraw-Hill, 2000.

Spence, John. "Small-Caps Are Hot, but Indexes Diverge." IndexFunds.com, April, 2002.

Swedroe, Larry. "Does Indexing Affect Stock Prices?" IndexFunds.com, March, 2002.

Tan, Kopin, "Covered Calls Grow in Popularity as Stock Indexes Remain Sluggish." *The Wall Street Journal*, April 12, 2002.

"25 Years of Indexing" by PriceWaterhouseCoopers, 1997.

Index